Love Is Greater
Than Pain

Love Is Greater Than Pain

SECRETS FROM THE UNIVERSE FOR HEALING AFTER LOSS

Marilyn Kapp

HARMONY
BOOKS

Library of Congress Cataloging-in-Publication Data

Names: Kapp, Marilyn, author.
Title: Love is greater than pain : secrets from the universe for healing after loss /
Marilyn Kapp.
Description: First edition. | New York : Harmony Books, 2020. | Summary: "In Love
Is Greater Than Pain, Kapp teaches us how to understand and interact with the
afterlife, using personal stories from her clients and from her own life, and transcripts
of actual channeling sessions. She explains in clear and simple language how our
well-being, growth, happiness, and actions directly impact our loved ones who've
passed. She even includes a chapter on communicating with pets after they have
passed. Death doesn't end a relationship or the love it held. By keeping the door open
and honoring life even as we grieve, we are able to continue to experience love and
healing, and even comfort our loved ones who have passed do the same."—Provided
by publisher.
Identifiers: LCCN 2019034892 (print) | LCCN 2019034893 (ebook) |
ISBN 9781984854872 | ISBN 9781984854889 (ebook)
Subjects: LCSH: Spiritualism.
Classification: LCC BF1261.2 .K367 2020 (print) | LCC BF1261.2 (ebook) |
DDC 133.9--dc23
LC record available at https://lccn.loc.gov/2019034892
LC ebook record available at https://lccn.loc.gov/2019034893

ISBN 978-1-9848-5487-2
Ebook ISBN 978-1-9848-5488-9

Printed in Canada

Book design by Meighan Cavanaugh
Jacket design by Jess Morphew
Jacket image by apiguide/Shutterstock

10 9 8 7 6 5 4 3 2 1

First Edition

To Harry

Our greatest gifts: Sarah, Jesse, and Zachary

My parents: Agnes and Sam Margolies

My teacher: Elie Wiesel

Don't be a prisoner of your own illusions.

—ELIE WIESEL

There are two ways to live your life.
One, as though nothing is a miracle.
The other, as though everything is.

—ALBERT EINSTEIN

Contents

Introduction

It is 1958. I'm two and a half years old, barely tall enough to see over the top of the bed, but that doesn't stop me from watching my grandfather rise up out of his body. He got up that morning, shaved, and dressed as he always did. Then he did something unusual. After his morning ablutions, he went back to his bed and lay down. I followed and stood next to his bed. That's when it happens. As he floats up, I can see that he looks the same as the body he is leaving behind. I'm not frightened. There's nothing scary about it.

In my next memory, a moment later, I am outside, standing on the front step of our house. The sky is blue with a few cottony clouds. I look up and see my grandfather rising higher and higher. He turns to me and waves, and I hear his voice assuring me that he will be back. As I watch him disappear into the sky, I am not sad. He said he would be back and I have no reason to doubt him.

He did come back, I'm not sure when, but before I have a chance to miss him. My grandfather continues to be a presence in my life. I sometimes see him sitting in the kitchen, in his usual spot. He smiles and I am happy.

. . .

As THE years go by, I start to realize that others do not share my perception. My mother wonders what her father might think about something, and I am puzzled. Why doesn't she just ask him? In an effort to be helpful, I offer to ask him, which I do. I feel happy to be the intermediary, as my grandfather is smiling and seems pleased when I ask him her questions. This type of conversation between my mother, grandfather, and me happens periodically, and my mother begins to sense my confusion. She explains that she can feel her father's presence and has always known that the loved ones who have passed are near and watching over us. I am happy to hear this because I can't even imagine how hard it must have been for my mother. Her mother passed when she was just nineteen. I'm surprised at what my mother says next. She tells me she cannot see or hear these loved ones, but she is happy that I can. Different people can do different things, she says, and she assures me that my ability is a good one.

I am determined to be the connection, the bridge, when my mother seeks her father's counsel.

My grandfather was almost blind in his later years. My brother, Mark, who is two years older than I, would take his hand and help him navigate. Mark offered his vision while my grandfather was in his physical body. Now that my grandfather has passed, I can offer my voice.

ONE DAY, when I am around seven or eight years old, I start to cry while playing cards with my father. He asks what is wrong. I don't want to tell him because things aren't making sense to me. My dad persists. I blurt out, "I miss Grandpa!" He hugs me and assures me that we all do. I don't know what to make of my feelings. How can I miss him while he is right here?

Over time, I come to realize that I miss his physical, in-body presence, the one who takes my hand and tells me stories. It helps that I still see him, though he is not appearing as often now. He seems to know when my mother or I have a question, and then he is right there, ready to communicate.

WHEN I am thirteen, my parents, my brother, Mark, and I have a family meeting. We are considering moving to a new home that is one town away. The biggest reason for the move is my unhappiness. I am bullied in school and in our neighborhood. Other kids don't know what to make of me, and I'm pretty uncomfortable in their presence. I'm distracted when I see or hear things going on around them. Though I know instinctively that I shouldn't share my reality, it doesn't stop the cruelty as the kids around me shut me out. Moving means I can start fresh and maybe figure out how to maneuver around people who don't already label me as "weird."

There is another factor contributing to my family's decision to move. Both my brother and I were born with eyes that looked in completely different directions. When we were ten and twelve, we had corrective surgery, but that didn't stop the teasing. I never questioned why Mark and I had this affliction. To me, it just supported my developing realization that one eye can be focused on this world, and the other can be seeing something else entirely. Though I know that this is not literally the case, I found it reassuring that my physicality represented who I am. I am still happy to have had the surgery; anything to appear less weird is welcome. If we move, the new kids won't already have this physical anomaly in their arsenal of things to be mean about.

My mother wants me to ask my grandfather if he will come with us. I love that this is a true consideration. My grandfather hears my mother, so I don't really have to ask. I laugh, along with my grandfather, as he explains that he is attached to the people he loves, not the place where he passed. My family is pleased and we make the move.

By now, I'm pretty clear that while my perception is considered normal at home, it is quite another story out there in my expanding world. I feel I have an opportunity to fit in, or at least try, and that means hiding a big piece of myself. I learn to be cautious. That doesn't stop the strange things I feel, see, and hear. I just know I shouldn't talk about it.

Sometimes, in other people's homes, I feel a sadness that is not my own. Other times, I feel anger or frustration. These emotions do not match up with what is happening for me personally, and I start to observe that others are not affected the way I am. I never know if or when this flood of emotion is going to happen and as a result, I continue to be socially awkward. Without constant vigilance, something might slip out. This is exactly what happens.

I am in high school and it is the end of the last class of the day. It is close to summer and the kids are all antsy, having a hard time focusing. We are given a few minutes of free time. I get up and change seats so I can talk to a classmate, a friendly girl I did not know well, other than to say hello. I ask her what her plans are for the summer. We are sitting next to a chalkboard, and as she answers my question, I pick up a piece of chalk and start to draw. I'm not really aware of what I am doing. She is excited about a babysitting job "down the Cape" (a Boston phrase for going to Cape Cod, Massachusetts). I am surprised when I see what I have drawn: a tombstone with "R.I.P." written on it. She looks at it and asks, "What is that?" In the same tone that I used to ask her about her summer plans, I reply, "A headstone." She points at the letters and asks what they mean. "Rest in peace," I calmly reply. "Who is it for?" she asks. Without emotion or shock, I look at her and say, "You." The bell rings, we say goodbye, and that's the end of it. My words didn't feel as if they came from me. I tell myself to be less weird.

The next day, people at school are unusually quiet. Everyone seems to know why, but I don't. I'm afraid to ask because that would just show everyone how strange I am. Conversations around me are in hushed tones, and some kids and teachers are crying. In second or third period our usually vibrant teacher solemnly tells us that today we'll sit quietly to meditate or do whatever we need to do. Halfway through the class, an announcement comes over the loudspeaker. The girl I'd talked to the day before has died. Apparently, everyone else already knew about the car accident that occurred the night before. Classmates around me burst into tears. I do, too. Such a nice girl, such a tragedy. Then I feel a jolt of horror as I recall our conversation. I am responsible! I have caused this!

The rest of the day is a blur. I am in shock and cannot begin to comprehend that kind of loss. I can't wait for school to be over and then for my mother to get home from work, so I can seek her counsel. She's barely in the door when I tearfully confess that I killed somebody. I go over every word of the conversation the girl and I had the day before. "Yes, I killed her! I didn't want to, but I did!"

My mother is not shocked by my words, though she is saddened by the loss of one so young. She calmly explains that there are energies that some people can feel, energies that translate to the receiver as emotions, even premonitions. I did not cause anything, my mother assures me. If anything, my strange behavior could have served as a warning. I listen and try to believe what my mother is saying, but I still feel responsible. In my determination to not cause any more harm, I vow to push this kind of energy away. I try to shut it down. Though I am determined, my resolution is impossible to achieve.

As TIME goes by, my "intuition" seems to be growing. Thankfully, it is not as scary anymore. Now it is taking the form of personal guidance. I accept this. At least I'm not hurting anyone.

IT IS now my first day of freshman year at Boston University. As I enter my first class, Hebrew language, I see a young man facing away from me. I experience what I now refer to as the "wave." Something big is happening. It's a warm feeling like a hug, but a chill at the same time. Like an internal, as well as an external, breeze, this energy wave feels like it is permeating every cell of my being. The young man turns around and I recognize him, though not from any memory I can recall. I instinctively know this man will be my husband. He catches my eye and walks past me as he leaves the room. His class is over and mine is about to begin.

I can't wait to go home and tell my parents. Because I'm a commuter, it happens the same day. "I know who I'm going to marry! I saw him and I know!" My mother does not seem surprised. With a smile, she accepts my declaration as fact. My father takes it in stride, too. If we are happy, he is happy.

A couple of my friends become spies as they help me determine a bit of the young man's schedule. My mother drives into Boston with me so I can point him out as he crosses the street on his way to class. Later, I call my aunt Celia in Florida to share my news. "I know who I'm going to marry!" She asks if we've gone out. The answer is no. Have we spoken? Again, I say no. She does not laugh, she does not doubt. She says that she is looking forward to meeting him. Celia is my mother's sister and I know she understands.

It takes a few months. Eventually, my unsuspecting target asks me to go out on a date. I hide my internal fireworks as I calmly respond. "This Saturday? Yes, that will work." I learn that his name is Harry. With his arms full of books, he maneuvers to open a notebook to take down my information. Suddenly, he straightens his arms and drops everything he is carrying! I am puzzled, but nothing can interfere with my joy. We pick up his books and con-tinue to make our plans. Much later, I learn that Harry's action was purposeful. By accident, he'd opened his notebook to the precise page where he had already written my information. He panicked, not wanting me to see it. It turned out that Harry had his spies as well, and one, without our knowing it, was spying for both of us! Harry had been watching me longer than I'd been watching him!

The summer before that academic year, we both would often go to the same beach where a lot of people our age congregated. Harry saw me, felt a connection, and would continually look for me over the summer, but was too shy to approach me. As summer drew to a close, he realized it was now or never. He tossed a football my way. I grabbed it and threw it back without a second glance. Harry was disappointed. That first day of school, when he turned and there I was, he thought, "God is giving me another chance."

Was I shocked when he told me this? Not really. It all made sense. I laughed as I shared with him the fact that I'm extremely nearsighted. I didn't have my contacts in that day at the beach. Vanity kept me from wearing my glasses, as they are pretty thick and, in my mind, unattractive. I didn't even see the person who threw the ball.

While others found our "how we met" story serendipitous, I took it at face value. Rather than being amazed, I am delighted that Harry and I seem to share a similar energy, whatever that means.

HARRY AND I date as we continue our studies. I major in communications. From the time I was young, I wanted to be an interpreter for the deaf. Though I don't know anyone personally who is hearing impaired, I teach myself some sign language. I am also interested in theater, especially theater for the deaf.

I realize now, in hindsight, that my early passions helped prepare me to channel for others. However unconscious, I seem to have had the desire and ability to interpret for others, whether for the deaf or for my grandfather, so that he could send his messages to my mother.

HARRY IS a senior the year we meet. He graduates and then continues in Boston University's MBA program. It is at this graduation that I first lay eyes on the man who will help me fully accept and honor my broadening perception.

Shortly before Harry's graduation, I had watched a play on PBS called *Zalmen, or The Madness of God,* written by Elie Wiesel. The play takes place after the Holocaust. Wiesel, a survivor of Auschwitz and Buchenwald, has Zalmen, the madman, open the play. He calls the town's rabbi "the defender of the faith, weak, pitiful, finding consolation only in tears." The townspeople form a tribunal to question God in the face of human atrocities. The rabbi defends God, stating: "God requires of man not that he live, but that he choose to live. What matters is to choose—at the risk of being defeated ... Death comes only later; it does not affect the choice itself."

The rabbi's words, and the play itself, had resonated deeply with me. I have a personal and conversational relationship with God that predates any religious training. It goes back as far as I can remember. I recall standing outside as a very young child, looking up at the sky and stating, "We'll laugh about this when I get home." I don't remember what I was referring to, but I know that the home I was referring to was not the house I lived in. Though I have always felt that God is my ally, I have some issues with God that I am not comfortable with. Why was there such a dichotomy between my realities? When people die, the resulting grief can be overwhelming; and yet, because of my perception, I know that life continues and it's not the end at all. I don't understand why there is so much sorrow and fear, yet I myself feel these emotions. I had a lot of questions for God and at Harry's graduation, here is a man, Elie Wiesel, who is not afraid to ask such questions openly. I am determined to meet this man who also struggled to understand God's intentions.

I don't have to wait long. I am elated when he announces that he is coming to teach at Boston University the following fall.

In September, I am a senior, so I am allowed to sign up for Professor Wiesel's class, along with several hundred others. The large lecture hall cannot contain the crowd of students. The professor enters the room wearing sunglasses. He takes them off and scans the faces peering eagerly at him. Our eyes meet, he nods, and he begins his lecture. There's no doubt about it. He looked right at me and yet I have a sense that everyone in the room is having a similar personal experience. My attention is then pulled to the group of out-of-body people surrounding him. I don't see them the same way I saw my grandfather, who looked pretty much the same as he did before he passed. The figures surrounding Professor Wiesel look like beings of light. They are shaped like human beings and resemble people in old photographic negatives. Their facial features are hazy. I am mesmerized and feel instinctively that they are fully conscious, and want to be seen. The focus of the class is the Literature of Memory, and Professor Wiesel speaks about the Holocaust. It feels to me that his out-of-body entourage is made up of people who passed in the concentration camps. He is their representative, their voice. I grow comfortable with seeing them and totally trust my teacher.

The semester continues and patterns emerge. Professor Wiesel and I acknowledge each other with a nod, he teaches, and I focus on his words while observing his out-of-body companions. But we have not yet had a personal conversation.

THE NEXT semester, Professor Wiesel offers a course that is more intimate. Fewer than twenty of us meet each week in his office. I don't know why I am allowed to attend, as he handpicked the students. All of us hang on his every word as he speaks of religion and philosophy.

My heart is as open as my mind. I know I have always been hungry for this sort of knowledge. Again, as Professor Wiesel teaches, I see the many people in spirit hovering around him.

One day, as Professor Wiesel enters the room, I feel a sharp pain in my right ear. Then Professor Wiesel addresses us, saying, "I was supposed to meet with Jimmy Carter in Washington. We're putting together a President's Commission on the Holocaust, but I couldn't fly today because I have an ear infection." Immediately, the pain in my ear is gone! Several weeks later, I find myself in an elevator with my teacher. My throat starts to throb. Wiesel turns to me and mentions that his throat is hurting. Again, after he acknowledges his discomfort, mine stops. I know I have to address this unusual phenomenon, but how? I schedule an appointment with him, and though I hope I won't sound crazy, I pour my heart out to him and share what I have experienced. I have only one line prepared as I end my nervous narrative: "So, please take better care of yourself because you're killing me!" At least I can try to make him laugh before he writes me off as being insane. Professor Wiesel laughs, but kindly. He asks me to tell him more about myself and my abilities. I am honored to share with him what he already knows: that a crowd of out-of-body loved ones always surrounds him.

He smiles and encourages me to embrace my gift, telling me that it can be used to help people. He assures me that my ability to connect with those who have passed is not an affront to any religion. In fact, he tells me that when he was very young, in his childhood home of Sighet, Romania, his mother and their rabbi spoke of these things. One day, his mother took him with her to visit the rabbi, who congratulated him on his dedication to his studies. Then, he was sent outside. A little while later, his mother emerged from the synagogue in tears. He did not know why at the time, but later learned that the rabbi had told his mother that her son would become a spokesperson, a witness, to what was to come. His mother fully believed the rabbi's premonition and it came to be. Elie Wiesel was a teenager when his life was uprooted by the Holocaust. He later fulfilled the rabbi's prophecy when he wrote the book *Night*, published in 1956, detailing his personal experiences.

After Professor Wiesel quietly shares his story, I feel a weight lifting. Again my dear teacher tells me not to hide from my perception. I realize that the rabbi was unable to stop the future horror that he perceived. I take a deep breath and fully understand that I did not kill that girl in high school.

When Professor Wiesel encouraged me to embrace who I am, I felt I had come home.

I GRADUATE from Boston University in 1977, and Harry and I are married that summer. Though I attend graduate school at Emerson College for a master of arts degree in theater, Professor Wiesel invites me to audit his classes, which I do for several years. He becomes a mentor to me. My parents, Harry, and I attend the three public lectures he delivers every year at Boston University. Eventually, I'm listening with a sleeping baby in my arms. Our son wakes up and is hungry. As I stand to take him out to the stairwell to feed him, Professor Wiesel looks over at us, nods, and smiles.

At that moment, I recall something that happened during his first semester at Boston University. Professor Wiesel was speaking when we heard a baby cry out in the hallway. This was unusual. The sound subsided and our teacher turned to us with a smile. I remember every word he said. "My son is two years old. When you have a child, every child becomes your child."

The years pass and our family grows. I continue to attend Professor Wiesel's public lectures, and we always exchange cards at the holidays.

I am growing comfortable with my perception and as a result, it continues to expand. I am being taught to be more efficient in translating energetic information. I feel the presence of guides, high-vibrational out-of-body beings. They channel in their intention to support our growth while we are both in body and out of body. Some people refer to them as angels, or guardian angels. Sometimes they present themselves and I channel them for people who are in need of their advice, though most of what I channel comes from loved ones who have passed.

I realize that my physical senses are being expanded and utilized in a broader way now in order to help me translate messages more easily. I perceive out-of-body people in several different ways. I still see them, though they look more like the beings I saw surrounding Elie Wiesel. I no longer see them the way I saw my grandfather, fully clothed and the same as he looked while in his physical body. I believe that I am being guided to use a form of energetic shorthand, allowing a broader, more efficient level of communication. What I don't see with my physical vision, I "see" in my mind's eye. This way, I can still describe facial features, which further verifies who is coming in to communicate. I can hear them. Though on a few occasions I do hear them audibly, I usually hear them inside my head. There are now full sentences and longer dissertations that I can repeat.

WHILE I am grateful that my perception is becoming more fine-tuned, I often have a dilemma. I don't know how to turn it off! I find myself distracted by whatever is happening "out there." I am startled one day when I close my eyes and see a plane crash. I observe the people who are leaving their physical bodies, and see their faces as they float up from the wreckage. It feels like I am an observer, like I am watching a TV screen. I'm shocked when I see the event covered on the news. It happened exactly as I saw it. Later, the faces I had seen matched the photos in the newspaper.

In my dismay, I recall my mother's advice. Perceiving things does not mean I caused them. With Elie Wiesel's help, I no longer have doubt. Still, if I'm going to see something so horrible, maybe I can find a way to help or stop it from happening. So I have a conversation with God, whom I also refer to as Divine Consciousness. I believe that all consciousness is connected to this Source, and this is the place I go for clarity. I ask that I be used as an instrument of healing, according to God's will. If I can be of service, if my perception can be used to help, then by all means, bring it on. But if something is in God's will and my perception cannot contribute to the overall good, I ask not to see it.

SHORTLY AFTER the plea for clarity and peace, I am in a car accident. I am in the front passenger seat when someone runs a red light and hits us broadside. I am the only one injured. Metal strikes the back of my head, and the impact causes my jaw to snap shut and chip my front teeth. I go by ambulance to a nearby hospital where they stitch the wound in the back of my head. The loss of blood and the surface injury are not big concerns. However, I have sustained a concussion.

I have never heard about post-concussion syndrome, but I learn a lot about it in the year that follows the accident. I have frequent headaches and often feel dizzy and confused. I can handle that. The tough part is that I am forgetting what I'm saying mid-sentence. I can't trust myself to speak clearly and often use the wrong words. The doctors are reassuring. It will take about a year for the symptoms to subside. During this time, I start to have a sneaking suspicion that my brain is somehow being rewired, but in a good way. I realize that my prayer is being answered.

A little over a year after the accident, the symptoms do subside, but I am different. I no longer see random scenarios on the spiritual plane. Now whatever I see has a purpose. I can deliver messages and leave it to the receiver to decide what to make of them. I develop confidence knowing that the channeling is totally aligned with my intention to serve Divine Consciousness and help people.

SOON, THE idea of protection and intention is channeled in. My desire is that everything I channel be for healing purposes. I align this intention by asking Divine Consciousness to make sure that all channeling be for the highest good and bring peace, insight, and healing to the recipient. I also realize that I need personal protection. This seems like an especially good idea, as my modes of perception are expanding. I can still see and hear people, but how

I feel inside myself is changing. Instead of the confusing flood of other people's angst, I can now discern whose emotion is coming through and the purpose it conveys. I literally feel the out-of-body person's or guide's energy in my body while I channel. Again, I feel I am being taught a form of spiritual shorthand. The words I hear, pictures I see, and sensations in my body combine to maximize the amount of information I can download and convey. While I channel, I may gesture or have the facial expressions of the one who passed. My body becomes a canvas of expression. I feel sensations that relay how someone passed, if this is the information they want to get across. If I feel a pain in my neck, I then discern the intended message, whether it's to convey a chronic physical malady, the way in which the person passed from the physical body, or if they are referring to someone, or themselves, as a pain in the neck.

I am growing more comfortable and realize that I love to channel. With clarity comes joyfulness. I palpably feel the relief of the out-of-body person as continued love and reassurance are channeled in. Whether the communication includes pledges of love or apologies for mistakes, the energy feels healing and expansive.

IN 1998, our family moves to California. I will not see Elie Wiesel's physical form again, but that does not mean we will not be together. In February of 2007, I have a vision. I can't remember if I was awake or asleep at the time. The communication takes place on the spiritual level. It feels visceral and real. Professor Wiesel and I are running toward each other. We embrace and he whispers, "It's okay, I'm okay." I come out of the experience relieved that he is okay, but worried that this might mean he has passed. I check the news and find nothing. A few days later, though, I read in the paper that on the night of my vision, Elie Wiesel had been attacked in a hate crime. Thankfully, he was not badly hurt. I feel grateful for that and also for our energetic connection. Once again, my teacher demonstrated that expanded perception provides reassurance and healing.

Years later, when Wiesel does pass, I am not surprised that it is on the anniversary of my father's passing. Wiesel had been delighted to know that my father was a direct descendant of the Baal Shem Tov, the founder of Hasidism, the Jewish sect that espouses joyfulness and a close personal relationship with God. I only learned of this family connection when I shared with my father what I was learning in Professor Wiesel's class about the Baal Shem Tov!

I AM now very comfortable seeing, hearing, and feeling those who are out of body. I am happy to channel for loved ones. Eventually, one of those loved ones pushes me to channel professionally. Robin Lippin, a friend from Boston University, has become a Hollywood casting director. She talks me into allowing her to share my name with a couple of friends. I will be forever grateful to her for giving me that push.

Word spread throughout the entertainment community. That was how, years later, I received a call from the actress Dee Wallace, who portrayed the mom in the movie *E.T.* She asks me if I might be interested in being a speaker on the Law of Attraction Talk Radio Cruise. Harry and I are grateful for this opportunity and the subsequent chain of events, including my channeling the answer to my own greatest puzzle. I'll share that story in Chapter 1.

I AM so grateful to be allowed to channel, yet I still grieve and miss the people I love who have passed. In the midst of pain and sorrow, it is easy to think that it must be so much better "out there." On the other hand, my recent struggle through cancer has taught me just how much I want to stay here on the physical plane. I have learned that we can integrate embracing our physical life here on Earth with the knowledge that our out-of-body loved ones still love us, and that they continue to learn and grow with us after they pass.

To help balance this apparent dichotomy, loving guides told me to sit down and take some dictation, and so this book was conceived. I am sharing personal as well as professional stories, in the hope that you will recognize the ways your own out-of-body loved ones are not just dear, but also near.

I RECORD channeled sessions. But while I'm grateful to have that resource, I don't really need it. When I focus on sharing a particular channeling session, the out-of-body person I originally channeled comes through. I will then rehear the parts of the session they feel will best benefit others. I write down their dictation only to find that they have supplied, word for word, portions of the original recording! Often, they will give an update and talk about how the communication has helped them and the in-body loved ones who received it. With their permission, I have included the newer messages along with the original channeled material.

In-body recipients of the channeled sessions are generous in allowing their experiences to be shared. I still think it best to change all names and identifiable information.

Now THAT I am channeling for a wide range of people, I ask that Divine Consciousness help me remember only the expansive concepts, love, and healing. After a session, I thank those who have channeled in, along with Divine Consciousness. I then let go of the personal details. In this way, the recipient of the channeling is assured privacy and I'm not taking into my consciousness what is not meant for me.

With this boundary in place, I am grateful to find that many of those I have channeled will spontaneously come in, sharing their experiences in an effort to help others. So while I might not remember details, the person who originally provided them may decide to come in again and share. They have also shown up in my times of need, during health challenges, to cheer me on and provide reassurance. The kindness and reciprocity they demonstrated during their physical lives are still part of their agenda, or maybe they have grown more empathic during their time out of body. I witness this generosity when I'm channeling for a group. A lot of out-of-body people will not just address their own loved ones, they might chime in to help someone they didn't previously know.

I am constantly astounded by the consciousness and kindness that surround us.

SOME OF the topics addressed here merit much further discussion, and some raise questions that I don't always know how to answer. Maybe your own experiences can further illuminate your understanding.

Professor Wiesel often told us that our job was to discover and ask the questions. We don't need to know or figure out the answers. As time goes by, I continue to realize how profound this concept is. If we limit ourselves to only the questions we can answer, we will never discover, or rediscover, our wisdom and grace, some of which may be lurking just outside our consciousness.

CHAPTER 1

Alan and the Secret
to the Universe

As thirty-two-year-old Alan lay dying from cancer, I stroked his chin. I told him I had always known that God creates people as beautiful as he was, but I had wondered if they were as beautiful on the inside. Now I knew. Alan smiled.

Fifteen months earlier, Alan was diagnosed with stage 4 liver cancer. It was a shock not only to him, but also to everyone who knew him. He was otherwise healthy, athletic, and filled with joyful enthusiasm. He loved hiking, surfing, traveling, and learning about the latest technology. He was happiest when surrounded by family, friends, and music. With a smile that lights up the room, his enthusiasm was contagious. He drew you in, whoever you were, and you became part of the party.

My introduction to Alan came through a series of events that I now believe was directed by a higher consciousness. It was on the Law of Attraction Talk Radio Cruise that my husband and I met Amean Hameed, an intuitive healer and a teacher. Amean's focus had been on energy healing, while mine was on channeling. Though we "downloaded" information differently, the results were complementary. Amean would focus his intention on healing and then magnify and direct energy where it was needed. Participants in his seminar reported relief of physical symptoms and an increased feeling of well-being. Amean's goal was aligned with mine, to relieve pain and suffering. We were delighted to discover that we had something else in common. We are both totally joyful when sharing what we have learned. This was the catalyst that drew us toward each other, as we offered to work together with the group's participants after our presentations were done.

I was not surprised to hear from Amean soon after we docked. He shared that his brother, Eamen, who was also an intuitive healer, had presented along with him on a previous Law of Attraction Talk Radio Cruise, but had chosen not to join him on this last one, as their loved one, Alan, had recently received that devastating diagnosis. Amean's hope was that we could all combine our energies and be of help. A date was set. My brother, Mark, and our friend, Betty Jampel, a social worker well versed in helping families through traumatic illness, were visiting us at the time, and they joined us.

Alan's mother, Fay, warmly welcomed us and introduced us to her mother and a few other family members. Alan, who had moved back home after his diagnosis, was too weak from chemotherapy to join us for dinner. The rest of us chatted, getting to know each other, and discussed Alan's prognosis. Though he willingly underwent all prescribed treatment, the doctors were not encouraging.

After dinner, Fay, Amean, Eamen, and I entered Alan's room. There, I saw resting quietly one of the most handsome men I have ever laid eyes on. His perfect features reminded me of a prince in a fairy tale. Alan opened his eyes and weakly revealed his trademark smile. We were introduced and I positioned myself behind him. He rested his head back against me. We all pictured light entering and healing his every cell, and I channeled the words of his grandfather and other out-of-body loved ones, who were in attendance. Alan was comforted and felt more relaxed.

HARRY AND I grew to know and love Alan and his family. Alan remained receptive to energy healing and channeling throughout his challenging medical treatment. He longed to be healed and stay in body as long as he could. At the same time, he approached the situation with curiosity and was determined to be as conscious as possible while navigating through uncharted territory. We got together often and also had weekly phone sessions that included Amean, Eamen, Fay, and other family members. Alan joined us when he had the energy; sometimes we did it while he slept. Amean would lead us in asking for protection from Divine Consciousness, and then we would direct our intention to healing. I continued to channel Alan's grandfather, who is Fay's father, and other loved ones.

Alan survived in his physical body for fifteen months after his diagnosis. The doctors were surprised, as their predictions had been much shorter. During the entire time, Alan's desire to learn was insatiable. He longed to understand and experience the spiritual plane as much as he could before he transitioned out of body. He felt that this would release his fear, as well as help all the loved ones who supported him on his journey.

ALAN REALIZED, through the channeling, that love surrounded him on every level. Not content to just hear about it, Alan wanted to learn if he could channel. I believe that this access is open to everyone. We would sit together and ask for protection from Divine Consciousness and then set our intention. We asked that Alan have conscious access to the spiritual world. Together we ventured forth. We did not question how we expanded beyond Alan's normal perception. We just knew we felt protected and calm. In a meditative state, I could feel, and see, Alan beside me as we visited the spiritual realm. His grandfather was right there, wanting to help. I watched as Alan's childhood dog, Wolfie, greeted him with boundless love. I laughed when I heard Alan audibly cry out for his mother. "Mom, Mom, Wolfie is here! I see Wolfie!"

YES, THE animals we love, and who love us, may choose to continue their relationship with us after they transition to the spiritual plane.

THIS EXPERIENCE dispelled any remaining fear Alan had about passing out of the physical body. My corroboration of what he had experienced while channeling further convinced him of his spiritual reality. I described his relatives and dog in detail. Everything matched what Alan saw. With his spiritual awareness open, Alan was ready for more. He asked me to leave the room so he could experiment with mental telepathy. He would project a message so that I could hear him in my mind and write it down. The first time he did this, he provided a long and heartfelt statement. When I returned to his bedside, he asked that I give it to his mother to be read at his eulogy. This practice helped Alan in his confidence that he would be able to channel through me even after he passed. He planned to do it a lot.

Even in the final days of his life on the physical plane, Alan's motivation to expand his consciousness, and ours, was front and center. This intention gave him comfort. I believe he realized fully that life was not going to be over. It was merely changing form.

A DAY or so before Alan passed, as he was drifting in and out of sleep, Fay and I stood on either side of him. Nothing else existed for us in those moments as we massaged him. Then Fay made an observation that astounded me:

"I never knew it could be this beautiful."

Fay was completely present—not in the past, not in the future—living through a parent's worst fear. Nevertheless, she could still see the beauty in Alan's transition back into the spiritual plane. Hearing her insight remains one of the most extraordinary moments I have ever experienced.

FOUR YEARS later, on the anniversary of Alan's passing, I told Fay that that one sentence changed my life. I was able to witness how consciousness and light can permeate even the darkest situation.

As I shared then with Fay, because I am able to channel, I can see the perfection and compassion of the Divine Plan. Within this system, life continues after physical death. Lessons are learned on the physical plane as well as on the spiritual plane, and it's all for our highest good. But there was one thing I didn't understand, one aspect I could not reconcile. Why, on this Earth plane, is there so much pain? I know that love never ends; we are never truly separated from our loved ones. In the big picture, everything makes sense. But here, on the physical plane, life is sometimes so hard. We can be overwhelmed with grief.

Alan, who was listening in on our conversation, as he often does when we're talking about him, presented himself. He was beaming; he looked radiant. He smiled at his mother, then at me. "I'm going to tell you the secret of the universe!" he channeled in. "It is this: to learn that *love is greater than pain*."

Alan was eager to tell us that when he had passed into the light four years earlier, the love was palpable. He saw his loved ones during his transition. He never felt separated from those he loves and who love him; his relationship just took a different form. Everything made sense.

SINCE ALAN'S passing, his mother has changed her life dramatically. After being Alan's primary caretaker for fifteen months, Fay felt that she could not go back to her successful corporate career. Instead, she wanted to share what she had learned during Alan's journey. She obtained a master's degree in social work and is now actively helping people at the end of their physical lives have a sweeter and more conscious transition.

Does she still miss Alan's physical form? Of course.

Does she still cry? How can she not?

How is she able to put one foot in front of the other and continue living?

She is able to do so by making a choice. The pain of having a child transition out of body is great, and often overwhelming. But Fay's love for her son, what he taught her, and what she is still learning with him are greater than her pain. *She does not deny her pain, but by recognizing that love is the dominant emotion, she is able to open her heart and actually feel Alan's presence and support.*

· · ·

ALAN REPORTS, through channeling, that his mother is helping him. They are actively collaborating to continue on a path together, a path of healing and growth.

Alan asks his mother, "Is your life better for having had me in it on the physical plane?"

"Of course!" his mother calls out in response.

"Then we are both better because of the life we shared. We will continue to be better, to make life better, and to share what we know."

WHEN WE focus on gratitude for the love we shared, even as we grieve, we open ourselves to the flow of love that continues. You see, death doesn't end a relationship or the love it held. It certainly changes our physical life. However, even after we pass, we continue growing and healing, even expressing humor. We, here in body, have the ability to consciously collaborate and support those who are now out of body. We do this not by shutting the door on life here on the physical plane, but by keeping the door open and honoring life. For those of us who are on the physical plane, recognizing and releasing our grief, opening our hearts to nature's splendor, and loving others, not only helps us but also our loved ones who have passed.

Yes, we can help them!

As we relieve and release our suffering, as we choose love as an active way of life, we collaborate with and help our loved ones who have passed. We watch for signs to confirm that they are with us. I believe that they watch for signs, too, confirming that we know they are with us, and that we are aware of their ongoing love.

When channeling, I often hear out-of-body children tell their heartbroken parents, "I cry when you cry!"

Do we need to cry? Of course we do. Will our tears and grief sneak up on us when we least expect it? That is a natural response. But when we acknowledge that both we, and our loved ones who have passed, are better for having shared our lives, we honor the love we shared, and become consciously aware that the love continues. Our love becomes greater than our pain and enables us to help ourselves, our out-of-body loved ones, and then, beautifully, those surrounding them and us!

If we didn't love truly and bravely, we wouldn't be in such pain when we suffer loss. The pain is the by-product of love.

ALAN IS proud of his mother, as she is of him. Their relationship continues to deepen and expand; and as they share what they have learned with others, they open hearts and minds to an expanded reality.

A MEMORY: Late one night, when Alan's transition was imminent, my husband and I left his bedside and went home. His mom, sister, uncles, aunt, and cousins were by his side. I was told that Alan wore his big trademark smile as he peacefully passed into light.

When I woke in the morning to a sun-filled room, I heard Alan's voice say loud and clear, "Good morning, Marilyn! It's a new day!"

I have channeled my whole life. I am used to "hearing" communication telepathically. But Alan's voice was audible. I understood that Alan's reference to a new day was not just about opening my eyes to God's earthly splendor. Alan was sharing his own reality. A new day, and broader consciousness, was his!

CHAPTER 2

Questions, Physics, and the Platypus

I n 1976, the *Boston Globe* wrote an article about Elie Wiesel's recent teaching position at Boston University. "Wiesel is much more comfortable with questions than with answers . . . In the beginning, he says, his students do not understand what he calls the 'arrogance of answers'. The professor is supposed to have answers. After a while they realize there is beauty in questions, more than answers. There is truth in questions. Questions never provoked a war, only answers'" (*Boston Globe*, October 3, 1976).

THIS PHILOSOPHY was the foundation upon which my perceptive abilities expanded. While I continued to receive information and counsel in nontraditional ways, I thanked God, but didn't look for answers. I took in and shared information as the gifts they were. I didn't try to fit the ability to channel into any preconceived notion of what perception should or should not be. From the time I was a child, I pictured jigsaw puzzle pieces floating down gently, one at a time, from the sky. Each piece represented something new to learn. For example, I began to realize that when I channel for people, their out-of-body relatives position themselves around those I'm channeling for in a very precise manner. A mother appears above and to the left of the in-body person, a father to the right. Grandparents present themselves slightly higher. A mother's parents appear above the out-of-body mother's spot, the grandmother to the left, the grandfather to the right. I see this configuration when I'm channeling for someone in person, and if I'm channeling over the phone, I close my eyes and see the presentation in my mind's eye.

My perception of this efficient alignment feels like one of the pieces of the larger puzzle. I picture each of these puzzle pieces rotating this way and that, as I understand and integrate what it is trying to teach me. As I grow comfortable and confident with the new information, I feel the piece softly click into place, integrating into the overall puzzle that is me. In gratitude, I look to the sky, eager for the next puzzle piece.

After I embraced my abilities and committed to their expansion, it felt that Divine Consciousness wanted me to learn quickly, but did not want to overwhelm or frighten me. I didn't need to know how it worked. I was comfortable adjusting to what I was taught. I think it served me that I didn't have the need for specific answers. I trusted that the questions were enough. I have observed that not limiting myself to my own or anyone else's answers helps me to not limit what is possible. I don't worry about what I know and what I don't know.

All of the channeling comes through with purpose and flows in quickly. That doesn't mean that I don't, once in a while, misread or make mistakes. One of the puzzle pieces helped me with this. If I see, hear, or feel something that the person receiving the information doesn't resonate with, I explain that I need a moment to stay with whatever is coming through. Those channeling in are purposeful in their communication. My translation or discernment may just need an adjustment. Whatever I am perceiving does not move on until I realize its context. For example, I might pick up that the person who passed had stomach discomfort while in body. I will feel that distress in my own body, thankfully not too uncomfortably. This stays until I decipher whether the person channeling in wants to relay a chronic stomach problem, a mild food allergy, or the idea that they couldn't "stomach" something or someone. I am patient and find that it is worth the extra few seconds to allow the context of what is coming through to become clear.

The receivers of channeled information tell me that what comes through is accurate and helps them heal, release old misunderstandings, and expand love. What answers would I need beyond that?

"And yet . . ."

I cannot recall a class with Elie Wiesel in which he did not speak those two words.

And yet, there are people who demand answers.

Questions expand us. Answers may fulfill a need for the logical mind, providing some respite as it categorizes what it is learning or can't explain.

I have always loved the platypus. Man categorizes; Divine Consciousness gives evidence outside the box of human comfort. According to an article in *National Geographic* from September 10, 2010, "[t]he first scientists to examine a specimen believed it was a hoax." But their conclusive answer to this conundrum was not correct. The platypus is a duckbilled, egg-laying mammal. It is real, regardless of the tendency of scientists to create artificial categories and to label what is beyond their comprehension as impossible. More questions, rather than an answer, would have led to an earlier understanding of the platypus and the unlimited genius of Divine Consciousness. It is amusing to note that after proper research, a *National Geographic* video describes the platypus as having "a sixth sense . . . radar, picking up vibrations."

I believe that science will eventually affirm that all of us have these abilities. Albert Einstein weighed in on the question about questions:

> The important thing is not to stop questioning. Curiosity has its own reason for existence. One cannot help but be in awe when he contemplates the mysteries of eternity, of life, of the marvelous structure of reality. It is enough if one tries merely to comprehend a little of this mystery every day.
>
> ALBERT EINSTEIN
> "OLD MAN'S ADVICE TO YOUTH: 'NEVER LOSE A HOLY CURIOSITY'"
> *LIFE* MAGAZINE (MAY 2, 1955), P. 64

As I write I hear Einstein laughing. This is not unusual, as I have channeled him for over twenty years. He has told me that he, along with other scientists and physicists, channels through many others as well, in order to provide guidance to those who continue his work.

Here is what he's channeling in:

We are always looking for answers. But the plausible answer leads to more questions. When we run out of questions, our thirst for knowledge is abated. Our inquisitiveness makes us human. We demand answers to our questions, but we should never be satiated by them. They should lead us to the next uncovering of what is not seen.

SEVERAL YEARS ago, I channeled for a couple whose son had recently passed. Before we started, the dad made it clear that he was only there to support his wife. He personally did not believe in channeling. His son seemed to take the bait and started the session by speaking directly to his dad. He provided information that could not be denied. He told his father how he sees him trying to hold back his grief, but then when he is alone, in his office at work, he paces, cries, and talks to his son. The father got up, paced, and cried while I channeled his son's words. The son went on to repeat, verbatim, the words his father said to him. No one else had heard them, just the out-of-body son. The mom smiled and quietly said, "I told you."

As the session went on, the son addressed other issues. When we were done, the dad hugged me. But then I was shocked by what he said: "I don't know. I just can't believe all this stuff."

The dad could not seem to allow what he had just experienced to disturb or disrupt the belief system that had given him answers in the past. It did not fit with the comfort zone his mind had created. There was no room for the platypus. Very real evidence could not, at that time, penetrate self-imposed limitation.

That is his prerogative.

I might question his choice, but if I label his behavior as right or wrong, I would be limiting my own perception of a fellow soul. His belief system is his own, and how he translates that for his use and growth is his business. I respect that.

As I write this, the son channels in to make a point. "My father may not have been able to wrap his head around the concept, but his heart knows. If his heart didn't feel my presence, he wouldn't have been pouring it out to me in his office!" I agree with him. His father's tears, as he affirmed what his son channeled in, revealed his deeper truth. His heart knew, even as his mind could not concur.

I LOVE the platypus, because however we choose to categorize it, it happily exists and goes on its merry way. It doesn't concern itself with our logic. That's how I feel about channeling. I haven't looked for logical answers, yet I believe that explaining the process the best I can may help provide access to those who would like to expand their own perception.

I've learned that many people channel without being conscious of doing so. Out-of-body loved ones often point out that their in-body loved ones react to their hugs, or start talking to them when they are near.

Guides channel in that we are all capable of feeling and interpreting a wide range of vibrational frequencies. We have the ability to raise our own personal vibrational frequency to align with, and gain information from, higher frequencies.

How do we do this?

When I ask, I am told that channeling and broadening our own personal vibration follow the laws of physics.

Channeling has come to feel so natural to me that hearing this makes perfect sense. The question is, does science substantiate it?

Think about the traditional scientific law "Matter can neither be created nor destroyed." Can energy be regarded as matter? If so, it fits with the idea that the energy contained in the human body does not simply disappear or dissipate when the body is no longer animated. Where does that energy go? It has to still exist. The proof is that it's possible for us, while we are still in the physical body, to channel information from the energy that used to inhabit a body like our own.

While there is not yet a scientific formula specific to this phenomenon, it is inevitable that there will soon be one. For more than twenty years I have channeled in that DNA is much broader than what science has discovered to date. Guides talk about a spiritual aspect of DNA that has a powerful effect on our physical health and well-being. Knowing about this can be helpful, they feel, in providing a deeper understanding of why we are the way we are.

For example, the trauma of our ancestors has a physical effect on our DNA and stimulates our adrenal system. This occurs whether or not the in-body person who is affected is aware of their ancestors' troubles. I channeled this type of information often, yet had no way to verify it. That recently changed when scientists expanded their research of epigenetics. So while I can't tell you exactly how expanding our personal vibrational frequency fits the laws of physics, I have no reason to doubt what I have channeled, and if it did not fit with these laws, I believe it would not be possible, or repeatable. In much the same way that science has now proven that spiritual and emotional factors affect DNA, eventually science will soon come up with a formula that maps out exactly how the laws of physics apply to channeling and the vibrational variations.

Albert Einstein did touch upon this.

A spirit is manifest in the laws of the universe—a spirit
vastly superior to that of man, and one in the face of
which we with our modern powers must feel humble.

WALTER ISAACSON, *EINSTEIN: HIS LIFE AND UNIVERSE*
(SIMON & SCHUSTER: 2007), PP 550–51

THE SCIENTIFIC equation is not yet known that will demonstrate
how it is not only possible but natural for a person to purposely
alter their own vibrational frequency to increase interaction with
other beings residing on different frequencies. I have no doubt that
it will soon be discovered. In the meantime, I will try to explain
how it all works to the best of my ability.

Science will catch up, as it did with the platypus and epigenetics.
Albert Einstein mirthfully comes in to channel an explanation for
why he did not focus on discovering this particular formula. "My
dear, I could not give an accurate report at that time. You see, I was
not dead!" Guides report that channeled information travels at the
speed of thought. Einstein channels in that eventually scientific
data will map this equation in correlation with time and space.

I HAVE experienced so much more than I can put down on paper.
No scribe could possibly capture in words the extent of what is experienced. This must be transferred through waves of energy, some
subtle, some not. Allowing our openness and setting our intention
opens the door.

Einstein channels in that:

Our work, from where we literally stand now, takes the
form of encouraging and expanding the minds and hearts

of those seeking knowledge. We work to save humanity and its home from the devastating destruction done by those who do not understand the subtleties of energetic expression.

What is the purpose of knowledge? To enlighten. While there is no guarantee that our help will be used proficiently, we choose, from our perspective, those who will best use the information constructively.

You see, **Humility is the key to Humanity**.

The personal ego cannot thrive at the same level as the altruistic soul devoted to the highest good.

For this reason, we are allowed to channel in a balanced and healing perspective that resonates with the receiver's desire to expand the mind and its self-imposed limitations.

Not everything can be seen. But magnetism exists as energies are drawn to like energies. Channeling is a way to decipher and align with the energy that can not only heal us, but can also heal those who are purposefully delivering it.

CHAPTER 3

Choosing to Raise
Your Vibration
After Loss

How can we possibly navigate through our lives after the death of a loved one when everything has changed? We are left facing a world that feels foreign and unfamiliar. We become disoriented in ways we couldn't have previously imagined.

I remember being shocked and angered when the seasons changed following my father's death. My world had shifted so dramatically that it didn't make sense for the earth to continue doing what it always did. In the days following my mother's passing I was caught off guard. I hadn't anticipated the dizziness I felt, as if the rug had literally, not just figuratively, been pulled out from under me.

It may feel unfair that we are expected to continue living and functioning in this physical world. Our arms ache to embrace our loved ones. We try to hold on to our memory of their voices, their quirks, their sparkle. The sun is shining, people are laughing, and we may feel detached, rooted in our own sorrow.

We need to understand that the trauma of the physical death of someone we love is something that we all eventually go through. However, knowing this doesn't help us when we ourselves are experiencing it.

Each of us processes grief and pain in our own personal way. Yet there is one aspect that we all share: grief depresses our energy and lowers our vibration.

Guides have channeled in that we are all ruled by the laws of physics. What does this mean? If we consider the human body as a vehicle, then the spirit, or soul, is the driver. This combination of physical and spiritual energies vibrates at a certain frequency. Our vibration fluctuates and resonates with our spiritual, emotional, and physical well-being. Physical death does not extinguish our energy or soul. Channeling reveals the soul's continuing cognizance, as well as the memory of the physical life experience. When souls leave the body, our out-of-body loved ones are just as viable as we are. They now reside out of the physical body at a higher vibrational frequency. They have access to us. Though we usually cannot see them, they can see us.

People often ask if their loved ones miss us the way we miss them. The answer is always a resounding "No." They may miss many aspects of the life they shared with us, but they're not wondering whether we still exist. They hug us when we cry. They hear our words. They long to comfort us through what we might believe is the final separation. They try, in very creative ways, to let us know that life is not at all final. Yes, it is the end of the physical life we have known together, but it's the beginning of a different type of communication. We can learn how to expand, how to be open to a broader vibrational field, one that is wide enough to "feel" and "hear" our out-of-body loved ones.

How do we raise our frequency? Actually, we do it all the time. A raised vibration is:

- That tingling feeling when we hear a newborn baby cry
- The silent awe we experience when we see a beautiful sunrise or sunset
- The wave of emotion we feel when we witness an act of loving-kindness or pure generosity
- The awakening we experience as we watch children discover the glory of the world around them
- The bliss or calm we feel when we take the time to meditate or simply to focus on our breath
- The peace that permeates us when we are at one with nature—when we listen to the ocean or a forest's hushed orchestra
- The inclusive joy and expansion we experience when participating in and appreciating the arts
- That incredible wave that comes when we know, just *know*, that along with our everyday life we are experiencing something more. We can feel it, in real time: a loved one who has passed is giving us a hug. Maybe they are drawing our attention to something that will comfort us: a song, a bird, a good-luck penny.

A raised vibration, when one becomes aware of experiencing it, is often accompanied by a chill or goosebumps. Horror movies take this sensation and run with it; they exaggerate it, trying to reenact the experience in a fearful way. While many find this entertaining, it is not what I have experienced. The communication I have channeled from loved ones who have passed may bring up a lot of emotions, but terror is not one of them.

Our out-of-body loved ones exist and are vibrating at a higher energetic frequency than we are. In order to feel communication with them, we need to learn to bridge the gap in a healthy and life-affirming way—by raising our own vibration. Does that mean we turn our backs on our physical lives? No. It's quite the opposite.

Divine Intelligence has set up an intricate educational system. Guides tell us that while we are residing on the spiritual plane, we do not have physical worries. We do not have to find a place to live, or a way to support ourselves. We are not dealing with and deciphering physical infirmities or experiencing the fear of "losing" someone we love. We have access to explore all the things that interest us. Souls are continually learning and expanding. For many this is enough. Others may desire more of a challenge to test themselves and further discover who they are. These souls bravely come into the physical body to experience the opportunities that schoolhouse Earth has to offer.

To help with this endeavor, we are equipped with a signal system that is integrated into the physical body. The actions and reactions of the adrenal system, the fight-or-flight impulse, the gut instinct that we experience in the stomach as nerves, butterflies, and so on, are among the many cues we can observe, alerting ourselves to what is aligned or misaligned with our soul's intention. If we pay attention, we can guide ourselves to discover what we have come here to learn.

Thankfully, science has come to recognize the mind-body connection and has also moved beyond the "blank slate" theory, the idea that babies come in without prior knowledge and preference.

The recently expanded scientific focus on epigenetics addresses how our ancestors' experiences have a profound effect on our physical makeup, inevitably influencing our emotions as well.

Through channeling, I have learned that there is another aspect to the consciousness we bring with us when we are born.

Soul Memory

Guides report that when the soul enters the physical form, it retains, to varying degrees, the memory of the out-of-body spiritual plane. Did you ever notice how babies look above our heads and smile and laugh? They are seeing the loved ones who were with them on the spiritual plane before they came here! Babies have high-vibrational frequencies that allow them to continue to observe and communicate with their out-of-body loved ones. This ability may last for years, and, for some of us (like me!), it never goes away. People often comment on children's facial expressions, or gestures, resembling those of a grandparent or great-grandparent who passed before they were born. The general consensus is that this is the result of genetics. But our out-of-body loved ones report that these similarities are actually a reflection of the residual memory of the time the future children and spiritual loved ones spent together on the spiritual plane before birth. So even if you feel you do not have access and cannot see or feel those on the spiritual plane, you *did* have this ability when you arrived on the physical plane.

Increasing our reciprocal communication with those in spirit is not a new endeavor for us. It's really about remembering what we are all capable of.

The fact that babies can't talk and share spiritual memories supports the soul's intention. For most of us, this stage is a time of transition as we turn our attention more fully to the physical plane and focus less on the spiritual plane. We are distracted by a colorful, brightly lit, and often loud environment. Embracing and learning how to make our way in the physical world usually becomes our sole reality. This physical reality provides the soul with the opportunity to grow.

Once we are born and living with others, we become self-aware or self-conscious. This is a necessary part of our development as we learn through experience that we have the power to impact our environment. It is normal to delight in cause and effect, especially when our efforts bring the desired results. As we grow and learn the ways of the world, we often become focused on what we can direct or control. In addition, we are being taught by others who have already become self-conscious, whether they are aware of that fact or not.

Ideally, we eventually realize that micromanaging limits us and becomes constrictive and exhausting. This is when we need and desire a broader consciousness to release us from negativity and stress. Combining what we are learning as our self-awareness expands with the consciousness we were born with leads us to our full autonomy.

To put it simply, it seems we come to the physical plane to forget, to some degree, the purpose of our journey. We challenge ourselves to rediscover, then expand on, our soul's desire. During this time, taking care of the physical needs of the earthly experience can be so distracting, we may think it's our only purpose and reality. Integrating this dichotomy between our soul's desire and the requirements of the physical plane is a learning curve we cannot access when we are out of body. On the physical plane, where there is so much to do, and so much to distract us, will we allow the logical mind and pragmatism to overtake our emotion or gut instinct? Will we find balance and resonate with our own autonomy, rather than base our experience on what others expect or demand of us? This is up to us as we go through our marvelous earthly adventure.

INEVITABLY, AT some point, we experience the loss of someone we love. The Earth plane may no longer feel beautiful; it may no longer feel like a playground for our soul's growth.

We have a choice. In our grief we may feel compelled to close the curtains and say "no" to life. We may even feel that we don't want to go on living. But our soul knows that our time and opportunity are not over on the physical plane.

How can we find balance?

When we choose and embrace the high vibration—the beauty and love that are available to us on the physical plane—we are led directly to the vibrational frequency where our out-of-body loved ones reside! It is through engaging with life, not denying it, that we maintain communication with our loved ones. This is how we are able to continue to experience love and healing, and help our loved ones who have passed do the same.

Isn't it perfect? We don't shut out life to reach our out-of-body loved ones—we embrace it. But how do we go about embracing life when we're grieving? When we feel we can't go on? First, we need to honor our grief, not deny it. And as we move through our grief we release the painful, yet inevitable, lower vibration that comes with it.

We will always miss our loved ones who no longer reside on the physical plane. But honoring them does not mean we should store our grief in our physical body. It's the love and the memories we want to hold on to, not the grief. Holding on to grief tightly, storing it in our physical bodies, can make us sick. This is the very definition of *dis-ease*. When we cry, share, yell, wail, laugh, then cry some more, it helps us release the heaviness. And as we let out our pain, our vibration rises higher. This emotional release allows us, literally, to be more closely synchronized with our out-of-body loved one's frequency. Will this alignment threaten our health or our lives? No. This is a natural and healthy state attainable through many modalities, including meditation, prayer, and the appreciation of nature and the arts. Remember, we all had this access when we were born. When we relax back into this state, we come to realize that we are surrounded by our out-of-body loved one's energy and love. It is physically palpable!

With this realization, we can allow ourselves to embrace life, all of life. We feel the impetus to complete our mission here on the Earth plane, knowing that we are not abandoned by those who have passed. In addition, as we raise our vibration and allow love to be the primary force, the power, and the choice, we help not only ourselves, but loved ones who have passed.

I would like to illustrate this by sharing a channeling session I had with a grieving mother.

Before channeling, I silently ask for protection for all of us and set the intention:

> We clothe ourselves in a robe of light, composed of the love, power, and wisdom of God.

We wear it not only for our own protection, but also so that those who see it, or come in contact with it, will be drawn to God and healed.

Please, God, let me be an instrument of healing as You see fit.

Please, God, guides, people who are here for God's healing, both in body and out of body, angels, archangels, ascended masters, help me to be a clear conduit.

Let the funnel open above my head as You see fit.

Help me to accept what does come in and help me to accept what does not come in.

Let me always be mindful of the sacredness of that which we do.

And please, God, let all that I do be Your will.

Over the years, this mantra has evolved. I encourage you to try it, incorporating your own personal belief system and using the language that best suits you. It is interesting to note that an out-of-body person channeling in will usually use the religious or spiritual terminology that they, and their in-body loved ones, are familiar with. Whether or not this matches my own orientation, the truth and light feel the same. Divine Consciousness and the expansive healing it brings are not limited to one ideology. Our personal religious background and preferred use of language can continue to provide comfort and be a strong affirmation when channeled in from our loved ones. Often, I'll stop while channeling and make it clear that I am not pushing any religious agenda. I'm reporting what the out-of-body person wants to share with us. So, this Jewish girl, while relaying that someone passed through the light of

Christ, honors the out-of-body person's intention and the universal spiritual reality. Whatever the language, it is real and represents the many manifestations of Divine Love and Consciousness.

As you read, take the time to pause, close your eyes, and feel your response. Reading and thinking about how to raise your personal vibration is actually one of the many ways to do it! Think about your own experiences. Right now your intentions are known. Your loved ones who have passed are surrounding you. They are eager to help you raise your vibration to facilitate continued communication with them and help you realize that:

Love Is Greater Than Pain

Isabel: I'm Here

When I met Sophia, I knew nothing about her other than what I could see. Her niece brought her to me for a channeling session. It had taken months to convince Aunt Sophia to meet with me. She needed support to walk and, although she was a relatively young woman, she looked much older than her years. She gave off an air of total defeat.

It didn't take long for a sweet girl, Isabel, who seemed to be about ten or eleven years old, to channel in. I could see her spiritual form right next to her mother. Isabel described her life and the circumstances of her death. The oldest of three, she had twin younger brothers. She reminisced about how she had always wanted to sit on her mother's lap and cuddle. Sophia's eyes grew wide and filled with tears as she whispered, "That's her."

Isabel longed to comfort her mother and tell her what had happened from her own perspective. She had run across the street without looking and was struck by a car. Several people had started screaming and run over to her. Isabel passed away before the ambulance arrived and before her mother could get to her.

Sophia had heard the commotion from upstairs and had run down as fast as she could. She quickly realized what had happened but didn't know it was her child who had been hit. As the people surrounding Isabel pulled Sophia forward, she saw Isabel's face and knew she was gone. She fell over her daughter's body and wailed, trying to protect her, begging her to come back.

Sophia's neighbors later told her that her daughter had still been conscious for a moment or two after the car had struck her, and that she had died right before her mother reached her side. Sophia had not been able to forgive herself for not getting there in time to comfort Isabel before she passed away. She decided that her daughter must be angry with her. Her grief was so deep that she could not function. Her younger boys went unfed, uncared for, and were eventually removed and placed in foster care.

Isabel, through channeling, pleaded, "Please, Mama, hear what I have to say. Hear the truth of what really happened! I ran out. I know you used to tell me all the time to look, but I saw my friend and forgot and ran out to talk to her. I'm sorry, Mama, I'm sorry. It wasn't your fault; you always told me! I felt a big push and a rushing noise in my ears, and then I didn't feel anything. Everybody started yelling, and I got scared. But I looked around, and Nanny was there smiling at me, and she was holding her hand out. Everything was all mixed up in my chest and stomach, and I couldn't stay there anymore. Then I heard, 'Here's Sophia, make room for

Sophia!' I wanted you to hold me and tell me, 'It's okay,' but I came apart from my body. I couldn't stay in there so I went with Nanny! I had to!"

Isabel was crying as she shared her experience with her mother.

"Don't worry, Mama, nothing hurt, I was okay. But I knew I had to go before I could look at you, because then I wouldn't want to go! I would want to stay with you and my body wouldn't let me! Mama, I left right before you got to me because I love you so much, not because I love you so little."

Sophia cried quietly as she listened. She had never thought of it that way. She had believed that her daughter hadn't loved her enough to hang on another moment. Sophia had brought her daughter into the world, and if Isabel had to go, she wanted to help her.

I felt Isabel's determination and strength as a surge of energy flowed through my own body. This was a girl on a mission.

"Mama, when you lost your daughter, my brothers lost their mother. Do you love me? Will you listen to me?"

"Yes, yes, sweetheart, anything you say!"

"Mama, I'm with you! I watch you! You don't eat right. You take drugs for all your pain. You're trying to die, to come to me, Mama. That's not right! I'm here. You're my mama. I won't go away. When you die, I'll be right here! You'll have your time with me. But then you'll say, 'My Isabel, what about my other babies, my boys!' And then it will be too late, Mama. Now is the time for my brothers. They need their mama! Do you remember how you used to make us healthy soup and lots of vegetables? We used to have fun cutting up and peeling fruit. Now you only eat junk that you wouldn't let us eat. Mama, that hurts me!

"You have a choice! I'm watching you, and it feels like it's my fault. Mama, I love you. Please, please take care. Take care of my brothers! Then, when you come to me, we will both be so proud! You can, Mama, please. I'm watching you. I'll stay by your side and help you!

"When you come, I want you to be happy, not mad at yourself. If you can't do it for you, do it for them, do it for me. Make me proud! They need you! I need you to be my mama and my brothers' mama!"

ONE OF the happiest phone calls I ever received came a few months later. The niece who had brought Sophia to meet with me called to say that her aunt's twin boys were returned to their mother, and together they were getting through each day and healing.

Sophia had had a choice. With her daughter Isabel's help, she made love the dominant driving force, above the pain that had fully taken over her life. Isabel, out of body, was desperate to help her mother and her brothers. She understood that her mother's feeling of helplessness compounded her pain. Sophia's realization that she could still help Isabel motivated her to take action. She now knows that her relationship with Isabel and her ability to affect her are ongoing.

The love continues.

CHAPTER 4

Life Review— Understanding the Reasons for Pain

Right now, as you read this, you are residing in the physical body. Grief is an active physical process that can be recognized, acknowledged, and released. To not honor and express our grief puts us out of balance physically and lowers our vibrational frequency. One of the challenges we face lies in our sense of helplessness. We cannot bring our loved one back onto the physical plane. Our frustration and sense of futility can lead us to express our grief through anger. We struggle for the illusion of control, to determine a cause and make sense of our loss. While this may be a natural response, and is inevitable at times, it is not healthy to be stuck in this emotion. Identifying the components of our anger helps us to consciously release it.

There are many ways our anger can manifest.

At our loved one who has passed:

- For being reckless
- For not trying harder

- For not loving us enough to "stay"
- For not listening to us
- For not staying home that day
- For not being more careful
- For not going to the doctor or for not going sooner
- For not taking better care of themselves
- For not realizing or caring that what they were doing was dangerous
- For being in the wrong place at the wrong time

If we are angry with our loved one, justified or not, we may realize that we are uncomfortable with that feeling. After all, our anger is a result of our love. If we weren't in so much pain from our loss, we wouldn't be angry.

We may then find it easier to project our anger in another direction.

To the doctors and the medical community:

- They said she had a good chance
- They told us, "If we did the treatment . . ."
- They screwed up
- They didn't try hard enough; they could have done something else
- They tried too hard, and the treatment made it worse
- They didn't catch it fast enough

To others who may have been involved:

- He got in with a bad crowd
- She had no right being with those people

- He wasn't watching out for her safety
- She wasn't taking good care of him
- The driver was intoxicated

And, of course, there's God, or acts of God:

- How could God let this happen?
- He's a good person, and God let him die
- I prayed, and God didn't listen
- Why did God allow that bad person to harm our loved one?
- God could have stopped that earthquake or extinguished that fire

The reasons for our anger can be endless. Whether or not our logic is valid, our anger turned outward gives us a place to direct our pain. Right or wrong in our assessments, we are releasing our emotion, even while we are helpless to reverse the situation, or even as we are directing our anger inappropriately.

Whether or not we can answer or have anyone else answer our questions does not take away our need to have a focal point. Pain from our loss may be so great that we feel we need the anger, on our loved one's behalf, to keep us functioning.

While anger is not always a helpful response to grief, as we may be deluding ourselves about its cause or using it to harm others, as we observe it, it starts to dissipate. We may come to the realization that our anger is not fully justified, or that it is not helping us. Rather than feeling guilty about our anger, we may find it helpful to acknowledge that we used it as a buffer to our trauma, allowing us to let off steam. We want to recognize our anger, but we don't want to hold on to it.

Enough research has been done on the mind-body connection for us to understand that prolonged anger has a negative effect on the physical body. If we can be clear enough to identify our anger, consciously examine it and release it, we have taken a healthy step toward our own healing.

Our out-of-body loved ones understand that anger is part of our adjustment period. Still, it pains them to watch us go through our pain on their behalf.

Anger Turned Inward

There are so many ways we can blame ourselves for our loved one's passing:

- I should have pushed him to take better care of himself
- I should have known how bad things were
- I should have made her go to the doctor
- I should have known what he was thinking
- I should have realized she was depressed
- I should have been there to prevent it
- I should have told him not to go
- I should have prayed harder

The self-recrimination can be endless. Whether or not our self-blame is truthful, it lowers our vibration and can make us sick or depressed. We don't want this for ourselves, and our out-of-body loved ones certainly do not want us stuck in that kind of pain.

Self-examination is necessary for growth. We learn by exploring and understanding our actions. But most of us are not complicit in, or responsible for, our loved one's passing. We have the capacity to understand that we turn our anger inward in an effort to make sense of the unacceptable. Though the reality is devastating, eventually we realize that we are not in control of everything and that it is not always within our power to change the circumstances and events around us.

When we are clear enough to sift through our thoughts and let go of the unfounded blame, we may be left with some anguish and true regret. We may be angry with ourselves over very real things we wish we had done differently.

- I didn't say "I love you"
- I didn't accept his lifestyle
- I rejected her partner
- I told him I never wanted to see him again
- I told her she was no good
- I couldn't take it anymore, and I wanted him to hurry up and die
- I didn't visit often enough

Acknowledging our true regrets and self-accusations is a very helpful and important part of healing.

"Why? What good is it to acknowledge our mistakes now?" you might ask.

The truth is: It is never too late!

We can pour out our hearts, tell our loved ones our feelings and our regrets, and share our sorrows with them.

Our loved ones are standing by. They are listening. They, like us, are wanting, even needing, to heal! They are walking with us hand in hand, helping us to heal and sharing their own healing.

You see, while we have been sifting through all the things we might have done differently, our loved ones are doing exactly the same thing!

Through channeling, our loved ones who have passed consistently describe going through a life review. While some people are happy to embrace this process, others report a reluctance to do so. Some may be angry that they passed when and how they did. Guilt and shame can push some to refuse to even look at the review. Souls are allowed to hide their heads in the sand, ostrich-style, for as long as they like. They tell us it may take days, weeks, even years, but it usually doesn't, because Divine Consciousness is clever.

People returning to the spiritual plane are surrounded by love and gentle guidance. They are encouraged to examine their life review, to understand the cause and effect of the many things we go through in life. If this is not enough impetus to bring them to examine their life, they're additionally promised that doing so will provide a way to help those left behind. Because love is greater than pain, the desire to help loved ones who still reside in the physical world usually overrides resistance and cuts through the guilt or shame.

Everything starts with love, even what may eventually end up causing us guilt or shame. We come into this world wanting to receive the love of those around us. Often, we'll mimic unkind and unproductive traits or behaviors to win the approval of those we love—for example, acting tough, not crying, or disliking other types of people. Then we perpetuate these behaviors, unaware that this goes against our own good nature and intention. During the life review we become conscious of this pattern.

Our out-of-body loved ones' review process mirrors our own self-examination, and sometimes self-recrimination, on the physical plane. They, too, observe that there were things they could have done better. Through channeling we learn that their biggest regret is usually not having shown enough emotion and authenticity. They recognize that they may not have expressed themselves in the way they intended or wished they had. They reexamine the life review with a deeper consciousness of perpetuated patterns. A father who has passed might be shocked to see that he behaved toward his child with the same aloofness his own father showed him. Even if we are aware of family patterns we do not want to perpetuate during our physical life, even if we swear we will not become what we abhor in others, we may slip into familiar behaviors without realizing it. Our role models have a lot of influence over us, even if we do not admire them.

Our loved ones are reminded of this during the review process, as most people are predominantly well intentioned. If the person observing his or her life review feels extensive guilt and shame, the review will then focus on the childhood wounds that may have led the person to shut down emotionally, or to become disengaged. Souls reviewing traumatic events in their life reviews are guided toward feeling empathy and compassion for the people they were on the physical plane. There is an understanding of cause and effect, and the door opens to the return of self-love. Witnessing the roots of the adult behavior we are not proud of makes it easier to forgive ourselves.

Once this is accomplished, the soul may be shown the roots of childhood pain of those who came before. For example, let's consider the man who did not want to be like his father. If he was abusive to his child, he will hate himself when he sees that part of his life review. He is then shown the way he was abused as a child by his own father. He wishes he could interfere by protecting his childhood self. In that moment, a couple of things happen. He has compassion for himself, even as he deeply regrets that he was unaware that he was projecting his father's pattern onto his own child. His heart opens to the potential to forgive, not just himself, but also the father who hurt him. The man is allowed to see his father's wounds and where they came from. Together, and enlightened, they can examine and release the pattern.

While we are encouraged to forgive others and ourselves during our life review, the healing does not end there. This man and his father can now take their conscious understanding and look to the son, who is still in the physical body, and help him to break the pattern and end the cycle of abuse. Most likely this man's own father is now capable of helping with this endeavor. Later, we will explore the many ways our out-of-body loved ones can help us, as they recover their authenticity and truth.

Remember, the best place to come to consciousness is in the physical world. When we examine our behavior and thought patterns, we can recognize how much was taught to us. We may need to examine and release some of our biases and rediscover our own true nature.

If this does not happen during our physical lifetime, the potential to do it is still clearly available to us after we have passed. We, who are still on the physical plane, can encourage our loved ones who have passed. We help ease their burdens and help them heal when we offer them our own perspective and love.

So here we are, loving and missing our loved one who has left the physical plane. We are processing, going over the past, reliving it. Those who have passed are processing along with us.

What happens when we bravely open our hearts and share our feelings with our out-of-body loved ones? What happens when a loved one receives this gift from you, a gift you may have thought was too late to give?

Bob's Story

It was almost twenty years ago when Bob, a high-level Hollywood network executive, came to me for a session. I knew nothing of his position, only that he presented as a warm and sweet guy.

He was open and ready to get going.

The first person to channel in was Bob's dad. When I told him so, Bob looked sad and said yes, his father had passed, but no, that was not who he was looking for. But I could only see his dad and did not perceive anyone else. I explained to Bob that his dad felt an urgent need to communicate. Bob shook his head. Clearly, he felt that his desire to hear from someone else took precedence. After his father insisted for a while that he had a message for his son, a very handsome man presented himself. He advised Bob to listen to his dad, saying that Bob would be glad if he did. Besides, the man pointed out, at the very least, once Bob's dad had his say, he would get out of the way! This younger man was obviously the person Bob wanted to speak with.

Bob reluctantly acquiesced.

DAD: Do you remember that six years ago, two years after I passed, you went into a room by yourself and said, "Dad, I just can't carry it anymore"? Bob, do you remember? You knew I never accepted your being gay. You tried so hard to please me. You just wanted me to love you, but I couldn't forgive you. Well, you sat in that room and said, "Dad, I love you and really hope you can love me. I can't carry this pain anymore. Dad, I forgive you and I hope you can forgive me."

Bob's father now had Bob's full attention. Bob explained to me that he had indeed gone into an empty room, and sat down to talk to his father. But the room hadn't been empty. Bob's father had just repeated verbatim everything that Bob had said out loud to him six years earlier.

The communication continued. After passing, Dad had had an opportunity to examine his life, and he realized that he had been wrong to withhold his love from his son. He had been taught to be biased. He'd learned from his elders that those with a different sexual orientation were unacceptable.

DAD: I understood after I passed how hard you had tried. You just wanted my love, nothing more. I felt so guilty. I felt I didn't have the right to watch over you and help you. But when I heard those words from you, I knew that our bond was not broken. I didn't have to be ashamed of the past. Your healing gave me permission to heal!

Bob's dad was proud of his son—of his integrity, kindness, and hard-earned success. Bob's generosity allowed his father to release his regret and shame. His father was overjoyed to hear that his love was welcomed.

OUR OUT-OF-BODY loved ones hear every word that is directed to them, anytime, anywhere. This is very different from overhearing or eavesdropping. I have never heard of this being an issue. Those out of body report that they hear messages that we specifically and intentionally offer to them. In addition, they tell us they are present and celebrating the events we desire to share with them, and they are present to help us through our grief and tough times. They are not looking to be inappropriate; their presence is aligned with loving intention.

BOB'S DAD then put his arm around David, Bob's significant other, who was patiently standing by.

DAD: You picked a good man. I'm sorry he passed. Since he passed, I have had the chance to get to know him. You chose wisely. I respect your choice, and I respect you. And with that I will leave you two so you can talk.

David was smiling. "Aren't you glad you listened?" he said to Bob. "Your dad told me he needed to go first, and when he told me why, I agreed!"

As Bob sat stunned, his dad retreated. His energy dissipated from the room. Bob then listened as David communicated with him for the next couple of hours.

BOB AND I went on to become good friends. I assumed, and he confirmed, that part of his determination to reach his high level of professional success stemmed from his dad's lack of acknowledgment. Yet all of Bob's accomplishments could not heal the pain of rejection he felt.

When Bob spoke to his father six years ago, he had decided that his love for his father, and for himself, was greater than the pain he had carried for years. He made a conscious decision that he no longer wanted to carry the hurt. He didn't care who was right or who was wrong. He just decided that enough was enough and that he had to release any negative emotion and only carry love.

Bob walked into that room thinking he was alone six years ago, assuming he was speaking to help only himself. He had no idea that he was gifting his father with the love his dad felt he did not deserve. By choosing love over pain, Bob eased his father's anguish and taught him that . . .

Love Is Greater Than Pain.

CHAPTER 5

Releasing Guilt Together—How We Can Help Each Other

We, and our out-of-body loved ones, are on a parallel path. As we are questioning everything we "could have" or "should have" done, our loved ones who have passed are doing the same as they go through their life review. When we learn how to clarify true regret and heal it, we can help our out-of-body loved ones recognize and release their regret as well.

Let's start with the guilt we may be left with on the physical plane. It is not uncommon to wonder what we have done to deserve such devastating loss. This type of thinking is amplified when there is a sense of responsibility for the survival and well-being of the loved one.

When a child is born, the most basic instinct is to ensure that no harm comes to this new and vulnerable life. As in most of the animal kingdom, a parent's purpose becomes focused on feeding, cleaning, and protecting offspring. While parents hope to instill self-sufficiency and independence in their children, that sense of being responsible often remains even through a child's adulthood.

I've channeled for many parents who have had children transition out of body, and the vast majority of them feel an overwhelming sense of having let their children down, whether or not they were in any way responsible for their passing, or even present when it happened. While it's logical to understand that an illness or an accident is not usually within a parent's control, the heart and the gut instinct may disagree.

- My love wasn't enough to keep him here.
- My prayers weren't strong enough.
- Life was too good. I didn't deserve to be this happy.
- I let God down.
- God hates me.
- Why didn't God take me instead?

We cannot minimize the devastating heartbreak of having a child pass. Yet it is helpful to hear what the children themselves have to say about it. Integrating their perspective into our own unifies the turmoil and reactive response of our mind with the truth of our heart. The heartache is the residual pain of having loved. Our instinct wants to recognize our heart's truth, that love doesn't just stop because the one we love is no longer physically available to us. It honors and helps our out-of-body loved ones when we openly acknowledge that our love continues. At the same time, those loved ones are trying to help us release our guilt.

Troy: I Sent You an Owl!

Dan came to the session alone. He presented as well put together and pragmatic. His composure slipped as soon as his young son came through. Troy was not yet two years old when he rolled off his parents' bed, became caught between the sheets and a nightstand, and suffocated. Dan had been on his way home from work and his wife had left the room for just a few minutes while her son was peacefully sleeping. When Dan arrived home, both parents went to check on their son. Though they desperately tried, they were not able to revive him. Dan recalled being in a daze as he stood outside waiting for the police to arrive, repeating the words "I'm sorry" over and over again.

Though Troy was not yet fully verbal during his physical life, when he appeared to me he was an excellent communicator. Children will present themselves at the age that they passed out of body. I believe they do this to allow accurate identification. Though I often see babies who are planning to come in to the physical plane, and babies who have returned to the spiritual plane, they do not seem to be trapped at that age. Picking up communication from a nonverbal child is not limited. I hear the words they would like to use to communicate, but because they are relaying an in-body experience that occurred while they were nonverbal, I will also feel the physical cues more acutely. Troy was determined to reassure his father and ease his pain. Through words, pictures, and sensations, he shared his own experience of what had happened.

TROY: I was sleeping and I was moving around, and then it felt all tight and I couldn't move. Then the front of my head felt tight, like my nose, and then I was floaty. Nothing hurt. I was floating all around. And you and Mommy got all scared. I was watching.

You love me! I know you love me! You got so mad!

When you went outside, I went with you. You kept saying "Sorry, sorry," and I tried to hug you. You couldn't see me so I asked for help.

Daddy, I brought you an owl! Do you remember? I asked for help and the owl came. You could see the owl even though you couldn't see me. I asked that owl to stay with you until the people came.

DAN: I thought I was in shock. I was crying and shaking my head and saying, "Sorry, I'm sorry," and I wiped my face with my hands. When I looked up, an owl was right there in the tree. That owl just looked at me. And it didn't move! It stayed there, it had to be minutes. I couldn't breathe, and then I could, and that owl was still there. Then the police came and I don't remember a lot after that.

TROY: Daddy, I brought you that owl because you couldn't see me! I'm okay! Daddy, I'm with you! I love you! That owl helped me to tell you! I'm not mad at you! I love you!

THOUGH WE are not able to understand why things happen the way they do, the love continues. When I channel, I am constantly reassured that we are loved and that our loved ones are aware of our distress and want to help us.

As I write this, Troy is communicating. He wants me to tell you this: "Daddy is still sad, but he looks up sometimes and says, 'I know, baby, I know, Troy.' He knows I still love him, and because I'm not mad, I think he feels better. He sometimes still says 'Sorry,' but then he says, 'I know!' When he gets here, I'm going to give him big hugs."

Our loved ones remind us that the love is greater than any guilt and pain.

Luke: God Is Not Mad at You

Luke was seventeen years old and always a good kid. He went to church with his parents, and though he could be a practical joker, he was never reckless. So it was a shock when he was found alone in his car after it hit a tree. There were no signs of drugs or alcohol. Though they weren't there when it happened, his devastated parents blamed themselves. After all, he hadn't done anything bad. God had to be punishing them.

When his parents came to see me, and I began to channel, Luke was eager to reassure his parents.

LUKE: Mom, Dad, I didn't do anything stupid. It wasn't anyone's fault. I just fell asleep. It wasn't your fault. You weren't even there. At first I thought it was my fault and I felt really bad. But everyone is helping me here. I didn't fall asleep on purpose. I don't want to make you sad. I love you! I love you, and God does, too! God is not mad at you! Mom, you always said that God loves me, and God loves you, too!

Mom, you love Mother Mary; you sometimes talk to her. Do you think God hates Mary?

MOM: No! Of course not!

LUKE: God wasn't punishing her when he took her son. Even

Mary couldn't protect her son. Mary is a good mother and so are you! If you could see the big picture, you would know!

Luke's mom sat quietly with tears running down her face.

MOM: He's right! He's so smart! It doesn't make sense that God would be mad at everyone who lost a child.

LUKE: Mom, if you get to stay on Earth longer, you can help other people to know. There are so many kids out here. Now I've become friends with some of them and we all feel so bad when people we love are mad at themselves. But don't feel guilty about feeling bad. I think it's kind of normal. It's just important to feel better.

Oh, and Mom, I'm not lost. I know where I am. I'm with you!

THE SADNESS, missing, and longing for the physical life we shared with our loved ones is unavoidable and overwhelming. Misconceptions we create through guilt and helplessness amplify the pain. Luke desperately wants to help his parents let go of the misguided but all-too-common notion that they are somehow to blame for his passing. He admits to them that after he passed, he also thought he was at fault. Guilt is not exclusive to those left behind on the physical plane. Thankfully, Luke is receiving loving guidance to help him let go of that fallacy and he, in turn, offers the same to his parents. Yes, they feel guilty, too, and we can help them.

This holds true not only for accidents. Many people struggle with health issues and try so hard to stay on the physical plane, yet they eventually pass, as the physical body is no longer able to hold them. They may feel frustrated because they were not able to fulfill the needs of those left behind and guilty that they let us down.

.　.　.

PARENTS AND partners, even when they have been unable to function well because of illness or advanced age, feel guilty about leaving.

- What will they do without me?
- They have taken care of me for so long! They will be lost without me!
- I need to hang on until the wedding, birthday, baby, etc.!

Children may feel that they let their parents down because they were physically unable to fight a disease. After passing, the children might feel that they were "bad" for going against their parents' wishes. You can remedy this immediately when you reassure them that this is not the case. Of course you wanted them to stay, because you love them, but of course it was not their fault.

Scott: "I tried, I really tried."

Scott appeared to be a healthy and athletic twelve-year-old, but all that changed when he started having headaches. Standard remedies offered little relief, and Scott's doctor set up further testing. The prognosis was grim. Several cancerous tumors were pressing on the nerves of his brain and causing the pain. Surgery followed to relieve the pressure. Radiation bought a little more time. Scott's parents and sister visited him in the hospital as often as possible. With each treatment, they reassured him that he was strong, that he could get through it. Their bond was tight, but it could not prevent the day when Scott could no longer stay in his physical body.

Scott's parents and sister came to the session eager to hear what he had to say. When they did, they were shocked.

SCOTT: I'm sorry, I'm really sorry! I tried! I tried so hard! I couldn't help it. I just floated out. It didn't hurt or anything. I didn't want you to be mad. But I couldn't help it. You were all there, and Nana. I stayed in the room for a while and everyone was crying. And then Dad got up and hit the wall. He was so mad. But then he came back and put his hand on my head. Remember? I was there watching. I wanted to tell you I was okay. Mom, you kissed me and said, "Scotty, I love you, be with the angels."

Then I saw Papa. I don't think you could see him. He hugged me and said I could go with him. And then Nana said, "He's with Papa now." Remember? She wasn't looking at us, but I knew that she knew.

With great emotion, Scott's mom, dad, and sister confirmed Scott's observations of his passing.

SCOTT: I didn't want you to be mad at me. I didn't do anything on purpose. I tried really hard!

I could hear Scott crying as he communicated through me.

Dad covered his face with his hands for a moment. Then he looked up.

DAD: Scotty, nobody was mad at you! We know you tried. You were unbelievable. I was just so mad because it's not fair. You're such a good boy, it's just not fair!

SCOTT: Dad, I know now, but I thought you were mad at me! Papa helped me, because I started to cry and I didn't know if I should go with him. He said it would be okay. It's because you love me, I know, but I really wanted to do what you wanted and I couldn't.

DAD (CRYING): No, no, you're so good! You're my boy! Oh God, you're so good!

SCOTT: It's okay, Dad, I know. And I think it's okay to get mad, but I just didn't want you to be mad at me.

DAD: Oh no, Scotty, I wasn't mad at you, I was mad at myself because I couldn't fix it!

I watched as Scott's energy embraced his father.

IT'S NORMAL to be mad. It's not unusual to yell at those we love who have passed, whether they tried to stay or not. It can help to let off steam and release our anguish. Remember, the anger is a by-product of our love. When we can acknowledge that, we not only help ourselves, we are helping our out-of-body loved ones.

How else can we help them? When I channel, I often hear:

"You told me it was okay to go. Thank you!"

I cannot overstate the gratitude that is channeled in as those who have passed relay how these words helped them. Sometimes they laugh and acknowledge that their loved one was lying to them—it wasn't okay at all. How could it be? But telling someone that it's all right to transition once physical death is imminent prioritizes the needs of the one who is leaving the body. Easing the mind of the person who is letting go is honoring the love over the pain.

The gratitude I channel in for a loved one's permission or encouragement to let go comes through to the bereaved whether the one receiving the words is conscious or not. The soul hears and understands. Those who have passed consistently channel in that they are cognitive and able to process what they hear, even if they are asleep, unconscious, and unresponsive.

Loved ones who remain on the physical plane are reassured, through channeling, that their words were not misconstrued.

> "You were trying to help me, and you did! I know you weren't trying to rush things, or get rid of me, when you said it was okay for me to go."

What if you couldn't or didn't say those words? There is still no reason for guilt. It is so comforting and important to know that an open pathway of communication and parallel healing allows you to clarify your feelings and make them known at any point in time. We can reassure our loved ones who have passed that:

- We know they did not intend to make us sad
- We know they did not want to let us down by dying
- We are grieving because we love and miss them
- We know that their love for us continues

This is all helpful whether it is acknowledged before or after the passing.

WHAT IF you are unable to honestly say or feel these things, either before or after your loved one transitions? You are not alone. Grief and sadness can be so overwhelming that it may be hard to experience anything else. Just remember that your grief and sadness are the result of loving and not wanting to lose someone you love on the physical plane.

Sometimes, when someone we love passes, we feel and grieve the loss of potential resolution. Maybe there is an apology in order on our part, or on theirs. So much of our emotional state mirrors that of our loved ones who have passed. Beyond the guilt surrounding the physical transition, they, like us, are reviewing our lives together. On this parallel path, we all may be taken by surprise by how desperately we feel the need to apologize and make amends for unfinished business that occurred during the life we shared. Like Bob's dad in Chapter 4, our loved ones are always available to receive our pleas. Hearing Bob's words was a catalyst for his dad's apology. Our communication remains interactive. All we have to do to ensure it happens is direct our attention and open our hearts. There's no special place to go, no special tools to buy, no special breathing exercises—all you have to do is look up and say, hey. Right here, right now. Deliver the message out loud, or telepathically, and trust that it is being received.

Dementia

My mom needed nursing care while going through radiation to treat cancer. She was almost blind and had advanced dementia. We were lucky to find a nursing facility with a memory-impairment unit near the hospital. Mom was the belle of the ball and won over caretakers, nurses, and fellow patients with her sense of humor, singing, and love for everyone she met.

I loved to be there with her. You couldn't find a more honest place. Dementia strips away so much of the ego and its inhibitions. Guides, and those who have passed back to the spiritual plane, report that dementia is a powerful tool for growth. So often we sublimate our true nature to accommodate the people or circumstances surrounding us. During wartime, financial hardship, or family trauma, a child may try to help, or hide, depending on the situation. Either way, the brain takes over to figure out the best way to maneuver successfully. The heart and gut instinct may take a back seat to what the mind prioritizes. A person may go through a lifetime not realizing that there is a pattern of suppression.

Dementia is the road back to full autonomy. The brain can no longer function the way it did in the past, and pragmatic thought can no longer repress emotions. It is interesting to note that those with dementia are usually very angry, or very happy. What is released when the mind can no longer perpetuate the unconscious façade is whatever was most suppressed during the lifetime.

If a child experienced trauma or abuse, there may have been little opportunity to delight in the magic and wonder of childhood. Appreciation of simple pleasures and playful interactions may not have been a priority or even possible. When the mind no longer positions itself as the control center, the soul is free to experience what the mind has been shutting out. The person is now available to enjoy the sweetness of the moment. It is literally an opportunity to have a second childhood. If a child has had a strict upbringing and was not allowed to express anger or resentment, this is what may be unleashed when the mind no longer has the ability to suppress it. Either way, the avalanche of emotion that the heart has repressed, whether consciously or unconsciously, will be set free to express itself.

How a person with dementia behaves is not random. Even if someone did not have trauma during childhood, dementia provides a path to loosen the chains imposed by the rigors of societal pressure. So many people have been taught to be seen and not heard. The focus was on accommodation and selflessness. Imagine the mind no longer playing by the rules. When I see a person with dementia cry or carry on, of course I have an empathic response. But I don't equate it with suffering. I realize that a lifetime of repression may be in the process of being released. If the person is bursting with joy in response to a hug, a puppy, or ice cream, I do not find their childlike nature to be sad or tragic. I see it for what it is, spontaneous delight that is no longer being suppressed.

One of the biggest gifts of dementia, I believe, is the opportunity to learn to receive. If people are brought up to provide for, and take care of, others, they find it easier to give than to receive. Growing up with a sense of obligation may further reinforce this imbalance. John Kennedy's famous words "Ask not what your country can do for you, ask what you can do for your country" stress the notion that giving is noble and receiving is not. While generosity is a wonderful trait, the flip side of it, gracious receiving, is also important. It has been channeled in many times that dementia breaks down the mental conditioning that taught us that it is impolite, or even selfish, to accept what is offered.

For many with dementia, the care they are now receiving is the only gentle nurturing they have ever received, or allowed themselves to receive. When the mind is no longer taxed with the idea of what one should be doing, or what others shouldn't be doing for them, people learn to accept help. Restoring balance in this way not only benefits the person with dementia, it helps the people who love them. After years of hearing "No, no, no," or "I'm fine, I don't need it," it's healing to have loved ones change their tune to sheer delight and acceptance of attention, love, and help.

This help comes from the spiritual plane, as well as the physical plane. When I would visit my mother, I would see the out-of-body loved ones lovingly surrounding patients. What's more, I often would see the patient responding to these loved ones, sometimes in a whisper, other times emphatically. Most caretakers and family members write off this type of behavior as a dementia-related psychosis. I believe that most of the time, the patients are responding to real out-of-body people in real time. As dementia clears the mind of what it no longer needs, it opens the door to spiritual communication. This makes sense to me, as all the ways to expand heart and gut energy to raise our vibrational frequency are happening spontaneously to the dementia patient whose mind appears to be shutting down. Without the distracting thoughts that all of us are subject to, the person's heart is completely available and present for all interaction and experiences. Deep, spontaneous healing has the opportunity to take place, transcending the physical plane. Out-of-body loved ones are clever and take advantage of the opportunities dementia presents. They will knowingly network and manipulate to bring about healing, for those in body, and also themselves.

Henry

Henry was new to the home. I was keeping my mother company during dinner when a nurse brought him into the dining area for the first time. He seemed a bit dazed for a few moments, and then his face cleared. He very deliberately walked over to a woman he had never met. She was seated and about to start her dinner when he reached down and took her hand. She was startled. As Henry held her hand, he looked into her eyes and said, "I'm so sorry! I'm so sorry for what I did. I love you and never wanted to hurt you."

Everyone was quiet, especially the caretakers. They were not used to this level of clarity in an advanced dementia unit.

The object of Henry's affection put her other hand over Henry's and gently said, "That's all right, dear. I forgive you. I love you."

I was sitting nearby with my mother as I watched this exchange. I saw more than what was visible on the physical plane. Henry's wife, who was out of body, was standing right next to him! I realized that she had led him to the in-body woman who would give him her desired response. I watched Henry's face soften as he let go of his burden. He sighed with relief as he was absolved. They let go of each other's hands, and the woman turned her attention back to her dinner.

In-body husband and out-of-body wife both relaxed, and their energies seemed to merge.

Business went on as usual in the dining room. The staff commented on the exchange. It was so sweet, but, of course, the men and women were strangers with dementia. The caretakers didn't realize or understand the beautiful orchestration on Henry's wife's part. She had wanted to hear her husband's confession and wanted it to be received with the love and forgiveness that she felt for him. I knew that when Henry's time came to pass, he wouldn't have to worry. He would be welcomed with loving arms.

. . .

LIKE ANY reciprocal conversation here on the Earth plane, honest communication between in-body and out-of-body people clarifies misunderstandings and lightens the heart. Our out-of-body loved ones are available to hear the words that will ease our pain. We just need to say them. Similarly, I can't tell you how often an out-of-body person channels in with anguish over the things they wish they had said. Patterns, pride, and lack of understanding are some of the reasons we may withhold the words of the heart. Once a soul has passed and is studying their life review, a lot of the intellectually constructed barriers fall away and consciousness is expanded.

Just like those of us who remain on the physical plane, our out-of-body loved ones want to love, forgive, and explain. They, too, may have that sinking feeling that it's too late. When the soul experiences this frustration, help is provided immediately. Guides gently assure the out-of-body souls that it is never too late to learn new modes of communication to reassure surviving loved ones. Those who have passed are learning that while the old methods of communication may not be available, love and intention will pave a new path.

Like us, they try to be brave as they adjust. Divine Consciousness is kind.

"Heaven wouldn't be heaven if I couldn't be with and help my loved ones" is a commonly channeled theme. They are here, and we are here. It is always interactive. It is good for us to remember this and act on it. Out-of-body children love to thank their parents for sending them a good-night kiss. The child feels acknowledged and is comforted to know that their continued existence is known.

Matteo: Still Following His Dreams

Matteo was always interested in medicine and looked forward to becoming a surgeon. Cancer changed that plan, but just on the physical plane. When it became clear that he would not be able to stay in his physical body for much longer, his mother, Rachelle, encouraged him to follow his passion and continue learning. She asked him to send her signs of his presence after he passed, but reassured him that with or without the signs, she would know that he was okay and doing his "work."

MATTEO: Mom, it's incredible! I can learn anything I want! I can watch doctors working on kids like me. You wouldn't believe how many people, like me, the way I am now, watch, learn, and help doctors while they are working!

It really helps that you talk to me every day and send me a kiss at night. Most kids are busy trying to get through to their families. That is their most important thing to do, and that's okay. But because you and I know we're still with each other, I get to have other work to do! Let me tell you what I have learned.

IT'S THE dance of energy, the dance of love, the dance of physics! We send love to our out-of-body loved ones and our own personal vibration rises. This results in more joy and a lighter heart for us here on the physical plane as we negotiate our own way. Our loved ones feel our love and, as a result, their vibration rises. All parties are lifted! Yes, we can help raise them up, just as they are doing for us. Our loved ones who have passed are actively sending their love to us, as they continue their own growth on the spiritual plane. Our consciousness of this truth elevates all of us! How? Raising our conscious awareness is the direct way to raise our vibrational frequency. When we are aware of the fluidity and fluctuations of our personal vibrational frequency, we tend to gravitate toward the stimuli that will support and help maintain a higher level. I believe that just thinking about raising our frequency is a catalyst to raise it. Guides report that we are literally applying the laws of physics when we think loving thoughts toward ourselves and others.

Einstein channels in:

> "Imagine how scientists will react once we have the formula that tracks the thought, time, space ratio! They will lift their heads from their microscopes, go to the nearest window, and allow the light to permeate all aspects of their beings. The jocular scientist will become the hero, as his previously unappreciated humor brings laughter and a pause in the mind's preoccupation with the task at hand. Better yet, each laboratory shall be issued a dog! Human happiness will prevail in the quiet and serious laboratory.
>
> "I can't help but wonder if the above recommendations are needed to discover the formula, or will be the results of the discovery.
>
> "Alas, once again it is the question of the chicken or the egg!"

Einstein wants to point out that if you laughed or felt joy while reading his musings, you have just done exactly what he is espousing!

Einstein continues. "You are now a genius! You are applying the formula, using yourself as the subject!"

Clearly we are applying the laws of physics, through our thoughts and actions and, even more simply and powerfully, through our intention.

You can practice this anytime. Close your eyes or look up, whatever feels more comfortable. What do you have to say to your loved ones? Maybe you are doing this for the first time, or maybe you are already having ongoing conversations. While you are directing your attention and love, maybe even your angst, to someone who has passed, notice what is going on in your body. Just relax and allow yourself to feel. Don't try too hard. Overthinking can get in the way.

REMEMBER, YOU came in knowing. As a soul inhabiting a physical vehicle, you can understand that while the mind might have trouble remembering this truth, your heart and gut do remember, and they delight in the expansion.

Elie Wiesel had a favorite quote that I return to when faced with a seeming dichotomy between the spiritual and physical worlds.

"Don't be a prisoner of your own illusions."

While this philosophy may be applied to many situations, it is especially pertinent when addressing spiritual access on the physical plane. We are spiritual beings, and as such it is not really logical that we would not have access to other spiritual beings just because at this point in time we are in a physical body. Yet, many people believe this to be true. If we are taught to be disempowered, if we are taught that we can't have access to spiritual reality, we may be led to believe that it doesn't exist at all.

If you have trouble aligning your mind to this idea, because it has been conditioned to accept limitations based on other people's illusions, then place your focus on your heart. Your love for those who passed lives on. Take a deep breath and allow your heart to feel the relief of that reality. All of your grief is a result of heartache. But the heart aches because it is loving and wants to be able to continue loving. I believe that part of the reason we feel so alone when a loved one passes is because we feel we do not have a place to put our love. Yes, of course there are many facets to our grief. However, feeling isolated and alone is an illusion we can dispel, even as we miss the many physical aspects of the life we shared with our loved one.

If you acknowledge the continuity of the soul, and you reject the illusion of the soul no longer existing just because you can't see it or because that's someone else's belief, then you are again remembering what your soul knows to be true.

The heart hasn't forgotten. Neither has your gut instinct. In fact, integrating the mind, heart, and gut to support the truth of this reality raises your vibrational frequency whether you desire to communicate with out-of-body loved ones or not. This expansion is part of our recipe for health, balance, and joy. Why would you limit your reality because other people limit theirs? Once you commit yourself, if you haven't already, to the truth of your birthright, you will find that your integration is contagious.

In the past few years, I have had a lot of medical care and intervention. Years ago, on the medical intake forms, I used to write "Consultant" in the spot for occupation. Not anymore. Now I open the door and write "Spiritual Medium." No one has rolled their eyes. No one has cracked a joke. In fact, just about everyone who sees my occupation listed will open up about a spiritual experience they had. So many people, whether they realize it or not, are longing to integrate and expand their spiritual knowingness within the logical reality of the belief system they have been taught. This makes sense. What could be more important than relaxing your whole heart and acknowledging the simple truth that life and love never die?

Elie Wiesel's quote does the trick on this issue. Being a prisoner to limitation just causes more pain. We can instead embrace our true reality, share it with each other, and collectively raise the vibration for all. Making the conscious choice and allowing the knowingness to wash over you as you take a deep breath dissolves the idea of a spiritual and physical dichotomy.

Every breath we take is mouth-to-mouth resuscitation with our energy source. That beautiful breath sustains us and is a constant reminder that for us, at this point in time, the key is to remain in the physical body and embrace the physical life around us. As we do, we can consciously absolve the guilt we no longer need to carry. When we address our loved ones with this intention, we find, beautifully, that it is reciprocated. Just as we send strength and courage to our loved ones who have returned to the spiritual plane, they do the same to help us continue to navigate our physical world.

CHAPTER 6

The Key to Spiritual Communication Is Embracing Joy on the Physical Plane

Eventually the love and beauty of the physical world will start to permeate the darkness of grief. The world is still turning—dogs' tails are still wagging, babies are born, birthdays are celebrated, flowers are blooming, and trees are growing. Realizing that normal life is continuing outside of our own circle of loss and grief can be jarring. We watch as family and friends, though saddened, return to their schedules and lives. Our idea of normal is now gone and will never be the same. We may be left realizing that to move forward in time will solidify the change in our lives. To engage in the now-altered world feels like a betrayal, a move away from our loved one who has passed.

But we have a choice! We can enter this new territory with broadened consciousness. Yet, how do we appropriately conduct ourselves when we know that our transitioned loved ones have access to us and can observe us? We want to remember that they are not eavesdropping. They report that our laughter is music to their ears. Our tears are often a call to action. They want to soothe us. They respond to our hearts' needs, when our souls call to them, whether we are aware of it or not. They are not hovering about, looking to judge our every word and action. They have their own work to do. Watching over us and helping us heal is a great part of what they choose to do and is encouraged by guides and Divine Consciousness for their healing as well as ours. This does not include spying on us. We can put our minds at ease on this issue. And we can ease their minds and reinforce their efforts by establishing a reciprocal way of communicating.

Allowing the physical world to provide comfort may feel counterintuitive to the desire to continue the relationship and communicate with our loved one on the spiritual plane. But it is really true. Acknowledging the beauty in the physical world that we can actually feel and touch is the necessary catalyst to raise our vibration. Without this awareness, our mistaken beliefs may lead us to imagine responses from our loved one that are not true. We might even create new rules for ourselves to accommodate our misguided thoughts.

- I'll never laugh again. I don't want her to think I'm having fun.
- If he sees me looking happy, he'll think that I don't care that he's gone.
- I don't want her to see anyone else pull me away from what we had.
- How can I enjoy my other children and move forward when one isn't with us?

Of course we want to honor the relationship we had on the physical plane. We don't want to "get over it" or "get past it." The thought of adjusting to our new circumstances may seem cold, as if we're purposefully leaving behind the loved one who has passed. But the truth is that embracing the beauty of the physical world literally moves us closer to the vibrational field of our loved one on the spiritual plane.

Let's look at the situation from the vantage point of those who have passed. Unlike us, they have conscious access, can see and hear us, and know for certain that we continue to exist. Through channeling, we learn that we share some basic concerns. They want to help us and are very concerned for our emotional well-being. Even as they experience their own sense of loss for what we had, they know beyond a doubt that love continues; that we will be united when our time comes to pass; and that the opportunity to acknowledge, resolve, and heal conflicts has not been lost.

Imagine their frustration as they try to reach out to us to ease our suffering. They want to let us know that though we are all resistant to change, moving forward is not only inevitable, but beneficial and even comforting.

The big picture is glorious! We shared a vibrational frequency with our loved one here on the physical plane and eventually we will embrace again when we are both within the shared vibrational frequency of the spiritual plane.

How CAN we best use the in-between time until we meet again? Our out-of-body loved one's desire for us is perfectly matched with what will best help us. Don't forget, we are in such pain because we loved. And we still love. Our arms long to hold them, our ears are hungry for their voice. Love, as the primary and continuing force in our lives, leads us naturally to raise our personal vibration. That vibration, which has been lowered by grief, fear, and helplessness, wants to correct itself. Our souls are happiest in the physical body when our vibrational frequency is high. As we know, the first step in raising our vibration is acknowledging and releasing our pain. Stuffing down that pain and plastering a smile on our face may fool a few people—and maybe even ourselves—for a short time. But denying our pain eventually stifles our joy, inadvertently extending the time we are experiencing the lower vibration. Recognizing and releasing pain, through crying, talking, hugging, even laughing, is essential to our physical and emotional well-being. Our loved ones are here for us, but they also know that for many of us, sharing with others in similar circumstances here on the physical plane can be a catalyst for releasing the lower vibration of grief.

While our loved ones shared the physical plane frequency with us, we were able to hug, talk, dance, and interact with each other. They know that we will be able to do all that again when we join them. But in the interim, our loved ones continually channel in their desire to help us value each and every day we have remaining on the physical plane. They want us to thrive. That means our continuing to hug, talk, dance, and enjoy people on the physical plane. They know that when we are engaged with the physical world, we are more open to picking up and processing that they are right here, right now, and looking to provide for us.

One message in particular comes through with great frequency when I'm channeling: "I love to hear you laugh!"

Yes, they want to lift our spirits because they love us, but they also know the role that physics plays. Our laughter raises our vibration closer to theirs. Does that mean that we are looking to leave our bodies? No, the joy and beauty of the physical plane can be both anchor and rocket! Laughter and connection on the physical plane grounds us and heals us, strengthening our body, which is our physical vehicle. Energetically, the laughter and connection lift us, much like meditation and prayer, allowing us to consciously experience and integrate the nonphysical higher frequencies.

Call it heaven on Earth. Our out-of-body loved ones want us to share this expanded reality. Their intention is not to rush us to join them—after all, they know that reunion is inevitable. Rather, it is to have us integrate this truth into our physical-life experience. This helps us release that hollow feeling of futility and enables us to open ourselves more fully to the time and opportunity we have available to us. When we understand that we will one day be reunited with our loved ones on the same vibrational plane, we can relax a bit. Even with our physical longing for those who have passed, we can make the decision to embrace those still here on the physical plane, along with Earth's magnificent bounty. Why not? Especially when we know that doing so helps ease the concerns of those who have passed.

Our loved ones in spirit want us to be better for the time we shared with them on the physical plane, not worse. Even if there are still issues to be addressed and resolved, love is most often the driving force. They will actively and creatively push us to embrace the love, beauty, and humor of the physical plane in an effort to help us regain our balance while we are still here.

My Dad

My father's health, along with his mental acuity, had been declining for several years. Still, we did not expect him to go so soon. The day before he passed, I brought our youngest child to see him. Sarah was ten months old and delighted my dad with her smiles and laughter. He was in bliss as he held her and talked to her. Though he didn't consciously know who we were, he was joyful to be with us.

As we got ready to leave, my father's mind seemed to clear. He made eye contact with me and said, "Come tomorrow at one o'clock." I was surprised by his lucidity. I later told my mother what he'd said, and the whole family came to see him at one o'clock the next day.

He had passed at noon.

I have never felt bad that we were not surrounding him at his bedside as he passed. It had felt as if his soul's desire had been clear and had come through in spite of his dementia. I believe he had not wanted to burden us with his dying—he had preferred to die alone.

Still, it was quite a shock.

Being able to see out-of-body people certainly has its advantages, but at times it can feel confusing. A couple of days later, as my dad's funeral was about to start, I saw a handsome out-of-body man with a full head of blond, wavy hair. My dad didn't have much hair, at least not while I knew him.

Channeling is quick and telepathic, so I acknowledged him and said, "You must be left over from the last funeral. I'm here for my dad." When I heard his bellowing laugh, I realized it was my father! He was clearly having some fun and projecting a younger version of himself.

When I later described the man I had seen to my mother, she found a photo of my dad in his army uniform taken during World War II. This was years before my parents met. There he was, exactly as I had seen him, with all that blond hair!

While I knew my father was with us, it was still hard to navigate his loss on the physical plane. Following the funeral, friends and family came to our home for the traditional Jewish week of mourning. Caring for our three small children helped Harry and me stay grounded and engaged. When they didn't need me, I found myself fixated on doing the laundry. Plenty of people were coming and going, paying their respects. But at quiet moments, I found solace in the ordered routine that doing laundry provided. I realized that repetitive physical chores helped to ground me and gave me comfort. I could control that laundry, even if I couldn't control the massive loss in my life.

Grabbing on to things we can control or find solace in is a healthy way to attach ourselves to the physical plane even as the physical world as we know it is collapsing. I believe it helps when we recognize this need. Focusing on the last visit with my dad and his insightful direction of when to visit the next day, and his youthful spiritual appearance at his funeral, gave me great comfort. Yet doing the laundry is what initially helped me to navigate my physical world during that devastating time.

WE MIGHT not anticipate, or even be particularly open to, the creative ways that the physical world can help heal us. It is helpful to remember, during these times, that often, a lifeline can come out of the blue.

Do You Trust Me?

Patty was devastated when her husband, Bill, passed. They had both had previous marriages, and children from those marriages, but only during their twelve years together did they feel that they were truly home. Patty is capable and smart and runs a business, but she loved that Bill would go to great lengths to have her feel that he was taking care of her. She came to me for a session, and after channeling in detail after detail of their life together, Bill stopped short and exclaimed, "Do you trust me?"

PATTY: Of course I do, Bill, always!

BILL: Don't worry how it will happen. I'm going to arrange it. Someone is going to offer you two dogs! Take them!

PATTY: What! Are you crazy? What am I going to do with two dogs?

BILL: Just listen to me! Please! You said you would!

THE CHANNELING moved on to other subjects. Two weeks later, a friend asked Patty to take her two young little pug dogs, as she could no longer care for them. Without Bill's instruction, Patty wouldn't have even considered it. She looked up to the heavens, laughed inwardly at Bill's high jinks, and reluctantly took the dogs.

Two months later Patty came for another channeling session.

. . .

BILL (LAUGHING): How do you like your dogs?

PATTY: They're crazy! The boy is always acting crazy, looking at the front door and barking at nothing!

BILL (STILL LAUGHING): Patty! He's not barking at nothing! I'm standing there! That dog is letting you know that I'm literally standing right inside the door! And speaking of the door, you're using it more!

PATTY, SUDDENLY REALIZING BILL'S WISDOM AND INTENTION: Oh, Bill, I didn't go out, I just stayed in and cried all the time!

BILL: It's good to cry, to let it out, but I think you forgot there's a world out there!

PATTY: I didn't want to talk to people, but now I talk to everyone when I'm out with the dogs. And those crazy dogs make me laugh all the time! Oh, Bill, you were right. You knew what to do!

BILL: Well, Patty, you listened!

Both Patty and Bill were laughing and crying at the same time.

BILL: Hey, Patty, together we're learning how to do this!

IT SEEMS remarkable, yet makes perfect sense, that our loved ones who are now on the spiritual plane know us so well. If we are open to their guidance, they will show us that we can be reunited with our own hearts, needs, and intentions. When we honor this truth, healing is multiplied as we bring our attention and love to those who still need us, right here on the physical plane.

Kerri: "Go to my brother!"

Joanne and Mike were loving their life. They had two devoted and creative children, and Mike's career was continuing its upward trajectory. He was now a full professor at a highly regarded university.

Their world was suddenly turned upside down when they received a call that their daughter, Kerri, while traveling with a friend, had been caught in a riptide and pulled out to sea. Her friend made it to shore and ran to get help, but when they returned, Kerri was nowhere to be found. Joanne came to see me for a channeling session.

KERRI: Mom! Mom! I'm here! I'm okay! It happened so fast. I was struggling because I knew what was happening. I took off my bathing-suit top and wrapped it around my head so people would be able to see me.

JOANNE: Yes! Yes! Your friend told us that she saw you do that! Kerri, you're so smart!

KERRI: Well, I thought that made sense, that people would spot me and rescue me. Then I was just so tired. I kept on trying. Mom, you have to know I tried. But then, I just felt this rush, the feeling that everything was okay. I could see you and Dad and I knew that I was okay. Then there was a lot of light and other people helping me.

I wasn't in pain, or even scared anymore. They showed me that I would be able to see you.

Mom, you have to tell Dad and Josh[her brother] that I'm okay.

I was watching when they came back to look for me. There were two boys swimming and going out too deep, but the people got them out. I'm glad they got there in time to get them out. But, Mom, I wasn't in my body anymore, and they couldn't find it.

JOANNE: Yes, they couldn't find your body.

KERRI: And, Mom, they never will! I don't want you to see that. I'm not in there and it doesn't look like me anymore, so I got help to push it far away, so you never have that vision in your head.

JOANNE: Oh my God, I was so relieved when they couldn't find you. I prayed they never would.

KERRI: I know, Mom. They help us out here with stuff like that. Mom, I love you, and I'm okay! I'm with you!

Kerri continues the conversation with her mom. She wants her family to be as happy as possible and celebrate the good things that are happening in their lives.

NOT LONG after Joanne's channeling session, Kerri's dad, Mike, felt it was time for his own session. The family was on the East Coast, so we had our conversation over the phone. After assuring her father that she was consciously with him and acknowledging his many accomplishments that took place since her physical passing, she became adamant that he needed to do something.

KERRI: Why are you on the phone doing this now when Josh invited you to his art opening? You can have both of us! We can continue this channeled conversation tomorrow. Right now, my brother needs to see his father walk through that door! And the reality is, if you don't go, when you get here after you transition, you'll look back and not understand why you didn't continue to honor your time with my brother when you had the opportunity.

Now is the time to do that! I'm going! I want you to be there for him. You do, too!

Joanne had just returned from the gallery, and Mike handed her the phone. As he ran out the door, I could see Kerri crying with relief. Her joy was palpable as she watched her father open his heart to celebrate his other child.

THE PEOPLE I channel for may be surprised when their out-of-body loved ones give them instruction or homework. But I'm not! This concern for us to maintain our loving connection to the physical world has been coming through in my channeling for years.

Imagine the frustration of our loved ones when they watch grief take over as the domineering force.

Riva

Riva was almost full term with her first child when her husband had a heart attack. Though help came quickly, he could not be revived. The shock put Riva into early labor. Fortunately, her son was born healthy. It was almost a year later when Riva came for a session. She told me that she had yet to look at her son, Jacob, without crying, and was concerned about his emotional welfare. She didn't want him to suffer as a result of her grief.

Riva's husband, David, was eager to talk to her.

DAVID: I'm so sorry. This is not what I had planned for us. I had no symptoms or I would have gone to the doctor. I went out of body fast. It didn't hurt. I was watching and saw those two guys working on me. If I could have stayed, I would have. There was a rupture in the upper-left part of my heart. The damage was too big.

RIVA: Yes, yes, we had an autopsy. David's right, it was the upper-left ventricle!

DAVID: Riva, I'm with you! I watch you! Please, we need to make things better. First, I'll really prove that it's me . . .

David described Jake's nursery in detail. He told his wife the names of the books she'd read to Jake the night before. He then went on to tell her that he understood her anger and grief.

DAVID: I get it, I really do. But you're focusing on what you don't have instead of what is right in front of you. Jake is so beautiful! Try to look at him, really look at him. He's right there in front of you.

RIVA AGREED to try, but only if we scheduled another session. David responded that he would agree to another session only if we put it off for six weeks. In that time, he instructed, Riva was to try to be as present as possible with her son, go out for dinner with her brother, go out with her friends, and go to a movie.

DAVID: Trust me, I really want to help you, and doing these things helps all of us. You can still grieve and cry, but you also have to do those things. Please, for me.

THOUGH RELUCTANT at first, Riva said she would. Six weeks later, I checked in with David and asked if he thought channeling for his wife was appropriate. He was happy to report that Riva had done her homework. We could do the session.

I was surprised when I saw Riva. She was focused and determined to show her husband that she had done all he asked.

RIVA: I did it! It wasn't easy. Everyone wants to babysit. That part is easy. I just felt so weird being out, like everything is normal.

DAVID: Your brother made you laugh! I saw it!

RIVA: I'm so sorry! I felt awful!

DAVID: No, Riva, I love you! I want to hear you laugh. I need to hear you laugh! We can't have what we want right now, but we have to make it good. Promise me you'll go out and laugh. Promise me you'll look at Jake and really see him. I'll stay and watch over you, but you have to stay with Jake.

DAVID CONTINUED to communicate and shared his hopes and dreams for his son. He also talked about Jake's development, proving once again to Riva that he was with them.

Riva's one wish was to have me channel David all the time. David wanted her to integrate her expanding spiritual knowledge into her day-to-day life on the physical plane. Again he gave her homework. A couple of months later, David came in to report that Riva was doing well and we could schedule a session.

This time Riva brought her brother with her, which turned out to be a very good thing.

DAVID: Riva, you're doing it! I hear you singing to Jake and smiling at him. Jakey is so happy.

RIVA: Oh, David, I'm doing it, but it still feels so weird. Sometimes I look at him and I love him so much, I'm just filled with joy. I'm so sorry.

DAVID: No, no, that's exactly what I want. Don't be sorry. When you're filled with joy, I'm filled with joy, too. We miss each other, but I see you, and you know that I'm with you. I'll prove it.

DAVID ASKED me to stand up, close my eyes, and focus all of my energy on him. I felt my dad, who had passed years earlier, coming in to help enhance and magnify the energy. I could feel David's presence become physically stronger. Riva and her brother both gasped.

RIVA: I see him!
    HER BROTHER WHISPERED: I do, too!
    After a few seconds, the vision dissipated.

DAVID: Now you know, now you really know! That took a lot of energy. We can't do that all the time. Believe me, we try. I'm glad you're both here, so you know it's real. You both saw.
    Now, Riva, you have your life here, in the physical world, and you have joy! You know that I'm helping and watching over you!

IT IS now several years later and David reports that Jacob has an in-body dad as well as his out-of-body dad. He also has a brother and a new baby sister! David continues to love his family and shares that he hugged the new brother and sister on the spiritual plane before they were born into his beautiful extended family.

CHAPTER 7

The Transition— Embracing the Spiritual Plane

Through channeling, we learn that our out-of-body loved ones are going through a process parallel to that of our own. They share in our grief for what was and what could have been. Though they miss the physical contact and the dynamics we shared just as much as we do, they can see us and spend time with us. They also know that at the end of our physical lives we will be joining them in the same vibrational frequency, just as they have joined those who have gone before them.

Love Never Dies; Love and Life Are Continuous

Clearly, our out-of-body loved ones are not wondering if we still exist and if we're okay. They know we exist and they're helping us to be okay. They also know that even though we may now be vibrating at different frequencies, love has no boundary and flows between us. We can reassure them that we share this understanding.

Our loved ones on the spiritual plane do not want us to be suffering alone. Even though they are with us, we know that they recognize the need for us to share, laugh, and cry with those who are with us on the physical plane. That shared camaraderie is tremendously healing.

Well, the same goes for them! We don't want our loved ones, who are passing, or who have passed, to feel alone. But we need not worry.

When I'm channeling for someone, I can generally see if a loved one is getting ready to pass out of body. If the transition is imminent, I will see a giant white tablecloth being flung out, toward me, over a huge table. Their loved ones on the other side are setting the table for the spirit's return, and they're gathering around. My understanding is that at the time of passing, our out-of-body loved ones are greeted by their loved ones—friends as well as family—who have previously passed. They recognize that when it's our time, we will be given the same reception; they now know for sure, from their own experience, that our time together is not over. Our loved ones will be there to embrace us when it's time for our own transition.

I love the metaphor of the giant tablecloth. The imagery relays our out-of-body loved ones' intention to receive us back to the spiritual plane with open arms and an eagerness to help us experience the transition with as much comfort as possible.

The idea of sitting at the table with those who have previously passed suggests a homecoming that we in body can relate to. As I write this, guides report that this greeting is really what does take place, though if we want food, the choice is ours. We do not require physical nourishment when we leave our body, because we are no longer sustaining it. However, this does not mean we can never have the experience of enjoying our favorite treats once we have passed back to the spiritual plane. We are allowed to manifest and delight in the foods that brought us joy when we were in body. So many out-of-body people channel in that the smells coming from the kitchens of their loved ones on the physical plane draw them in like a magnet. What makes us salivate in body can still tantalize us when we are out of body. I'm told that there are some people out there on the spiritual plane who don't want to be bothered with this. I won't be one of them! And I am particularly pleased that my father, diabetic while in body, can go to the deli anytime and indulge in the soothing comfort foods of his childhood. When I join him, I will start with an egg cream soda.

My Dad

I usually brought the kids with me when I visited my father at the hospital. He loved seeing them, though he no longer knew who they were and didn't know who I was, either. He was diabetic and had just had an ankle-to-groin vein replacement. The anesthesia needed for such a long and intricate procedure exacerbated his already advanced dementia. This one time, I visited alone.

Dad was sleeping, so I pulled up a chair and enjoyed just being near him. When he opened his eyes, he looked at me with clarity and recognition, something he hadn't done in years. He was completely lucid as he enthusiastically shared the experience he had just had.

"I was in this wonderful place! My brother was there, my father was there, and everyone knew me! I was there with Murray, and we wanted to stay. It was like we could just sit down and get comfortable and talk with everybody! They told us that we couldn't stay, but that we would be coming soon, not to worry."

My father's face was filled with joy.

"Uncle Murray?" I asked. My father's sister was married to Uncle Murray, and though they lived a few hundred miles away, we stayed in touch.

"No, no," my father replied, "Cousin Murray!"

"What? Cousin Murray?"

"Yeah, yeah, Cousin Murray! We both wanted to sit down and talk to everyone, but they wouldn't let us! But they said, don't worry, we'd return soon!"

I was taken aback by so many things about this conversation. It was the most coherent I'd seen my father in years. And who was Cousin Murray? I recalled that my father had a distant cousin named Murray, whom I had met only twice at extended family gatherings over thirty years earlier. I had not heard of or seen him since.

I asked again, "You mean Uncle Murray?"

His frustration could not undermine his excitement.

"No! Cousin Murray! It was great! My father and all his people were there!"

Dad elaborated a bit more and eventually fell asleep still smiling. I was incredibly grateful for my father's joy, and thrilled that I had been there so that he could share it. I marveled that he had had his experience the one time I had come alone.

Dad seemed to be in a deep sleep, so I left the hospital and went to my parents' home to pick up the kids. I told my mom what had happened and asked her about Cousin Murray.

My mother was also taken aback. She and my father hadn't been in touch with that branch of the family in many years. As I was leaving, my mother stopped me. "Wait a minute, let me call them." My mom got out her phone book and called Cousin Murray, who lived several states away. His family was astonished when my mother relayed my father's experience.

"Murray is in a coma!"

Both Cousin Murray and my father passed within a few days.

How kind they are out there! As my father was starting to let go of the physical plane, his loved ones on the spiritual plane made sure that he felt taken care of and loved. His heavenly preview eased any fear he may have had about his transition.

ELIE WIESEL often said that there is no such thing as coincidence. I believe this is true, especially when I think about how much energetic intention and influence come from our loved ones who have passed. I marvel at the degree of orchestration it took to manifest the beautiful experience that I was allowed to share with my father—the synchronistic timing, my dad's lucidity. His joy was pervasive and contagious. Though I would grieve his physical presence after he passed, it allowed me to know beyond a doubt that he was happy and surrounded by loved ones.

My father's surprising lucidity at the end of his life is a phenomenon I have seen with other people who are preparing to transition. My father's brain had been deteriorating for years. It was heartbreaking to see an image from a CT scan the doctor shared with us of the cumulative damage caused by prolonged diabetes. We had witnessed the consequences every day, as my father could no longer manage simple tasks. Yet, when he had his vision of spiritual reality, he had no trouble with word retrieval and sentence structure. He sounded like the father I knew in my earlier years. According to doctors, this would be impossible. His physical brain was no longer capable of performing at a cognizant level.

People with advanced dementia, brain injuries, or even in comas report through channeling after they have passed into the spiritual plane that they processed every word that they physically heard before passing. But their brains were not in charge of this "hearing." Though the brain is a wonderful computer, our memories, even the ones we can't recollect, are the soul's domain. Out-of-body people often laugh about that when they are channeling in. They point out that they left their physical brains behind, but they can share the events that happened both before and after their physical passing.

This knowledge is comforting in so many ways. First of all, everything we have learned and will continue to learn in this lifetime will go with us. Growth and wisdom are not wasted and discarded at the time of physical passing. In this light, futility has no place in our psyche! Secondly, our loved ones have a scrapbook of our shared experiences in their memory. When they pass, all of that stays with them. It is always accessible to our loved ones on the higher vibrational field. We can tap into that field through channeling and other communication modalities with the surety of knowing that when we are reunited after our own passing, we will have access to, and the ability to share, our loved ones' memories.

Our soul's intention overrides other physical limitations as well.

Some of our physical senses may appear to be shutting down as we near transition, only to be compensated by the soul's expanded perception.

MY MOTHER, in her later years, lost almost all of her vision. She also had advanced dementia (yes, both parents!). She could no longer identify any of us. The only time she used my name in her last few years was to ask me where Marilyn was. That's why it was so astounding when, a couple of days before she passed, she was lucid in a way that did not seem possible. A dear friend had come to visit us. She went to my mother's bedside and tenderly tucked the blanket around her. My mother's physical eyes were closed and we both thought she was sleeping. But, clear as day, with her eyes still closed, she said, "Thank you, Enid." Even more surprising, it was the first time in many years that she had pronounced Enid's name correctly.

Of course this makes sense, our loved ones on the spiritual plane tell us. They watch over us and see what's happening without the eyes they employed while in their physical bodies. The soul animates the physical vehicle but is not limited to the body's capabilities.

Our loved ones who have passed want us to know that as we near transition from the physical to the spiritual plane, it is possible to bask in the energy of both worlds or vibrational frequencies. People may sometimes hang on for days while absorbing the love from everyone around them. Though they may not appear conscious, they can hear, see, and feel their out-of-body loved ones right there, ministering to their physical and emotional needs.

Imagine the extent of our loved ones' comfort and joy, as they are welcomed by their loved ones who have passed before them.

I witnessed this both when my father shared his spiritual experience and when my mother was preparing to transition.

My Mom's Passing

In her eighty-eighth year, after uncomplainingly dealing with cancer and dementia, my mom was getting ready to pass out of body. The kind nurses and administrators where she was receiving care allowed me to stay with her during the last ten days and nights of her physical life. During that time, she was consciously aware of both her physical and spiritual visitors. She greeted my out-of-body father with enthusiasm yet told him that she wasn't ready to join him. Her eyes, nearly blind on the physical plane, focused upward: "Sammy! Sammy! No, not yet, come back tomorrow!" she told him. She lifted her head and with intense concentration and a broad smile listened to my in-body brother play the clarinet. Bill, her brother who passed years ago, made her laugh when he pulled on her toes. I looked at the foot of the bed as she wiggled her feet and giggled, "Bill, stop that!" and could clearly see his spiritual form. She agreed that this was a fitting gesture from a fun-loving, prankster podiatrist. It was a gift to share in her joy as she embraced the energy of those in body saying goodbye and those out of body saying hello.

When my mom was ready to leave her body, I was cuddled close and holding her hand. My eyes were closed, but I was fully awake. Suddenly I heard many voices and felt surrounded by bright golden light. I kept my eyes closed and could feel myself being lifted, along with my mother, into the embrace of loved ones. They seemed so excited and happy. My mother's delight was palpable. Then I felt a gentle push as I was guided back into my physical body.

My mother had passed.

I opened my eyes and turned to look at my husband. He had had his eyes open the whole time, and I'm so grateful he had. Filled with wonder, he shared what he had seen. He told me that both my mother and I had been resting quietly. Suddenly, we both lit up with the biggest smiles, and our faces filled with joy. Harry was able to see the physical reaction to our spiritual experience. We both looked at my mom's now-uninhabited body. She looked completely peaceful. Still partly in channeling mode, I continued to hear the ongoing spiritual reunion as loved ones greeted her.

My husband and I stayed still and present for quite a while. The energy in the room felt sacred. I realized that I had experienced this vibrational frequency before—it had permeated the room during every birth I was witness to, including those of my three children. We are held, loved, and bathed in light whether we are coming or going.

How beautiful to know we are not alone. If a loved one passes, even if there is no one with them on the physical plane, they are still not alone. That's an important thing for us to know, especially if we cannot be with our loved one at the time of their passing. So many of us hope to midwife our loved one through the physical-to-spiritual transition. Alternately, many of us find the thought of doing so hard to handle and would prefer not to be present. It shouldn't be surprising to learn that our loved one who is getting ready to transition may have strong feelings about this as well.

I've channeled in over and over that loved ones will hang on until certain people make it to their side. They, like us, long for a touch, the sound of a voice, or words that will bring comfort. With that reassurance, they can peacefully let go.

But just as often, I've channeled in the exact opposite! So many transitioned loved ones report that they actually waited for everyone to leave the room before they left their bodies.

"I love you too much to go!" is a common theme. Like Isabel in Chapter 3, who as a child was hit by a car and who passed right before her mother could reach her side, many people don't want to face going with those who have already passed—those who come to welcome and direct them—if their physical loved ones are present. If they do not yet realize that they will have access to their earthbound loved ones, they may feel that they are being asked to make a choice. Our out-of-body loved ones consistently report that while things might be rough leading up to transition, the actual passing from the physical body back to the spiritual plane is not painful. I am told that they are allowed to stay with us for up to several minutes if we are with them when they pass. If we are not physically present, they are able to come to us, and even embrace us, before they go off with the spiritual loved ones who are there to greet them. Every situation is unique. Sometimes, as in Isabel's case, the hug might be too difficult in that moment.

Please don't add to your guilt if your idea of how your loved one's transition should happen is not what transpires. It is helpful to allow our love to be greater than our pain by acquiescing to our loved one's agenda and supporting their needs.

So many times I have channeled in the following to people who are filled with guilt:

> "Thank God you finally needed to go to the bathroom. I couldn't hang on any longer."
> "They kept saying, [name] is coming. Try to hold on! I knew I had to let go. I love her/him too much to depart while they're here."

I believe that my father was doing exactly what he needed when he told me we should all come the next day at one o'clock. He passed an hour earlier. It makes sense to me that a parent would continue to be a parent and might choose to protect not just themselves from pain, but their children as well.

As for my mom, during those ten days that I was with her, I gave her the opportunity to go without my being present. Every day, I told her that I was going for a walk, and if she felt more comfortable transitioning without me there, I would understand. Of course I wanted to be with her, but I felt that the choice should be hers. Understanding that we are not in control of someone else's agenda can relieve any residual guilt we might have about not being present as a loved one leaves their body. Be kind to yourself. Allow your love to be greater than your pain as you recognize that your loved one who is transitioning may have a will of their own.

We also have to acknowledge that there may be circumstances in which we, and our loved one who is transitioning, do not have control. Sudden trauma or illness may take all choices out of everyone's hands.

Joe's Arrival

Carly and Joe had a long marriage and three children. Their youngest passed at age two from meningitis. Many years later, Joe passed suddenly from complications following heart surgery. Carly came to me for a channeling session, eager to hear how Joe was doing.

JOE: It didn't hurt, honey, really it didn't. I was asleep and then my mother was there holding her hand out to me. I looked down and saw my body lying there and that's when I knew. I asked my mother about you, and then I could see you at home, and I hugged you. I watched you. You caught your breath, and you knew, even if you didn't know. And that's why you weren't surprised at all when the hospital called. You felt it! Carly, look!

I could see Joe holding up a beautiful two-year-old boy. The child was presenting himself at the age he'd passed, looking like he did the last time Carly had seen him on the physical plane.

JOE: Look, Carly. John is here!

I described the boy to Carly as she cried.

CARLY: That's him, that's him. That's what he looks like!

JOE: We're still a family! He's been with us the whole time! Don't worry about us. We're fine! But we both want you to find at least one reason to smile every day. When you get here you can tell us about your adventures. You still have things to do. But you don't have to worry about us.

YOUR LOVED one is now out of body. Newly transitioned, our loved ones realize that they can travel at the speed of thought. Where do they go? I have heard it described in many ways, usually aligning with the belief system of the person who has transitioned.

- I went through the light.
- I passed through the light of Christ.
- There were guides, beings of light, who hugged me and told me not to worry.
- Everything made sense. I saw and felt the meaning of everything.

However it is conveyed, whatever words are used, I see and feel the exact same thing every time I speak to someone who has recently transitioned. While it makes sense that our loved ones out there use the language that they and their family identify with, the experience is universal. With bright light, loved ones, and an overwhelming feeling of being known and loved the sweetness is palpable.

∽✖∾

WHEN WE realize that life is continuous, we can release any sense of futility. After a loved one passes, it is very easy to succumb to thinking, "What's the point? If we die anyway, why bother living?" If we're only conscious of the physical plane, it seems like everything we learn and accomplish ends here. When we are feeling depressed, this can lead us to become disengaged with the physical world. When someone we love goes out of body, we may no longer have the impetus to continue living or take care of ourselves.

"He can't see it anyway."

"What's the point now that she's gone?"

When we consider the inevitability of our own passing, it helps to realize that we will not only be examining our life on the physical plane during our life review, we will be interacting, if we choose, with the loved ones with whom we shared that life. Those who have passed channel in that they can choose whether or not they want to spend time with those who have passed before them. If someone was abusive during their physical life, they may be in a rehab-type setting on the spiritual plane. There's plenty of therapy out there to help unravel motivations and behaviors that were not healthy. During this time, out-of-body people may not be available to channel to people on the physical plane. Guides and others close to them may report on their progress. More about this later.

Our out-of-body loved ones report, through channeling, that we have soul families. Like wolves, we travel in packs, helping and sometimes challenging each other to grow. Soul families can include family members, friends, even people we have only brief encounters with. Soul families usually have members in body and out of body at the same time. The connections of the soul are not severed when someone leaves the body.

Our loved ones who have passed often channel in the analogy that they have gone to the vacation house on Wednesday while we will be arriving on Saturday. Do you think that our loved ones don't care about us on Thursday and Friday? They are very invested in our well-being, happiness, and growth during that time and hope that their time with us before their Wednesday departure helps us through the physical separation. When we arrive on Saturday, our loved ones embrace us and want to hear all about our lives from our point of view. And of course, we'll want to hear all about theirs. What they've been doing and learning matters to us as well.

But there is more to this analogy. On Thursday and Friday, our loved ones also have access to us, and those of us on the physical plane can learn how to expand our communication with them. It's like having phone or video time. Would that communication take the place of interaction on the physical plane? Of course not . . . our loved ones consistently report that though they were able to see us, they still take great joy in later hearing about our Thursday and Friday adventures. And we can look forward to their sharing the revelations and expansions that they experienced on the spiritual plane during that time.

So, as we embrace the communication and connection with our loved ones who have passed, we also need to embrace the physical vibration and world we are living in. We wouldn't want our out-of-body loved ones just sitting in a chair waiting for us to get there. We want them to embrace everything that Divine Consciousness has to offer. When we show them that we are processing our grief, engaging with the physical world, and actively seeking joy and a higher vibration, we encourage them to do the same on the spiritual plane.

We're each going through a similar process. Guilt and grief are released as we encourage each other to expand and understand that nothing is ever lost and everything does matter.

CHAPTER 8

Collaboration: Interpreting Messages from Our Loved Ones

As we continue along a parallel path with our out-of-body loved ones, we will start to recognize the manifestations of our connections to them on the physical plane. Since our well-being, peace of mind, and health are of the utmost concern to our out-of-body loved ones, the assurances we receive of their care for us need not be a one-way street. When there is conscious collaboration on both sides, the magic and miracles happen. Like Bob, in Chapter 4, who went into a room, physically alone, and forgave his father, you can reassure your loved one anytime, anywhere. *Remember, you don't need a medium or an intermediary for your out-of-body loved one to hear you.* Often, as a channeled session comes to a close, the in-body person asks me to tell their out-of-body loved one that they love them. I tell them that in telling me their wishes, they just told them themselves!

Along with love, you can offer healing, appreciation, humor, and forgiveness.

Through channeling, our out-of-body loved ones report that they share the same intention. They purposefully align their energy with the vibrational energy of the physical plane to communicate with us and draw our attention to their continued love and concern.

If they could, our out-of-body loved ones would sit down and write us a letter, or, better yet, physically manifest. As we saw with Riva's husband, David, it takes an extraordinary amount of energy to manifest because their vibrational frequency is so much higher than ours. Therefore, we need to be observant, as they can be very creative in their efforts to reach out to us.

Electricity vibrates at a higher frequency than we do but at a lower frequency than that of our out-of-body loved ones. One way they manifest their presence and let us know they are with us is that, with effort on their part, they can flick the lights or turn the TV on and off.

Ethel and Elliot

Ethel was married to Elliot for more than sixty years and was having a hard time being alone after Elliot was moved to a nursing home. She could feel her parents with her, even though they had passed many years before. Often she would go into her bedroom at night and find that the light on the nightstand on her side of the bed was on. Ethel grew comfortable with this. She had never lived alone. As a young woman, she had gone from her parents' home right into her marriage. During his lifetime, Elliot, when he was well, was quite talkative. After Ethel acknowledged that she was having a hard time with the home being so quiet, the TV started going on in the middle of the night, even though the remote control was not on the bed. She wasn't frightened and instinctively felt that her parents were trying to help. She asked them to lower the sound when they did this, but that seemed to be a subtlety they could not master.

The weeks went by and the communication continued. On the night after Elliot's passing, Ethel went into her bedroom and found that the lamp on her side of the bed was not on. But the lamp on Elliot's side? That one was lit up.

It is especially comforting to receive a message in times of need.

A few years after my mother passed, I was diagnosed with invasive breast cancer. The surgeon was not encouraging. When my husband and I got home from the doctor's office, I sat on the bed, looked up, and asked my mother if I would survive. The TV turned on! We were nowhere near it, and the remote was on top of a dresser. Clearly she believed the answer was "Yes!"

Digital technology has an even higher vibration than electricity. Out-of-body people showing up in digital photography is not uncommon.

"I'll Be There"

Joan's son, Ben, was engaged to be married. Unfortunately, her husband, Jeff, had passed a few years earlier. She came to me for a channeling session.

JOAN: Please, just tell me if Jeff knows what's going on, if he can come to the wedding.

JEFF: Are you kidding? Of course, I'll be at the wedding! Wild horses couldn't keep me away!

JOAN: Can you give us a sign that you're there?

JEFF: I'll tell you what, you're taking lots of pictures, right?

JOAN: Of course! We hired a good photographer.

JEFF: Okay, here's what I'll do. I'm going to show up in the pictures! And other people will, too! We'll look like balls of light, but you'll definitely see us. You'll see white balls of light floating in the pictures. When you're standing up there with the wedding party, I'll be next to you, and you'll know it's me because I'll be a blue light! There will be a blue light next to you in the picture!

JOAN CALLED after the wedding when she received the photographs. There were several orbs of white light in the pictures of the guests dancing, appearing next to, or on, those whose significant others had passed. In a picture of the wedding party, next to Joan, was an orb of blue light!

∞

I HAVE witnessed this type of manifestation in my personal life as well. Three months after my mother passed, our family gathered for a holiday celebration. We all lined up for a photo. Next to my brother was a ball of white light! Of course I knew that my mom was often with us, but here she seized the opportunity to let us know that she is still enjoying the party.

Over the years I have seen many pictures of this type of manifestation. Those out of body report that it is much easier to present themselves as a ball of light rather than trying to appear as they did when they were on this plane. The high frequency of digital photography, they say, helps make this type of projection accessible.

Digital music devices—for example, cellphone and MP3 players—also provide a means of spiritual-to-physical communication.

Set your music on shuffle and ask your out-of-body loved ones a question. Be patient, as they're just learning how to operate this high frequency. Once they know how to use it, they will choose the song that best relays what they would like to tell you. They may even take over your entire playlist! For example, several hours after my mother passed, Harry, my brother, Mark, and I went to the car to drive home. Mark, a musician, put his MP3 player on shuffle and said, "Let's hear what Mom has to say." I could feel that our mother was still getting oriented and was not yet available to communicate. "Okay," Mark said. "Let's hear what Dad has to say!" Out of the sixty thousand or so pieces of music on his device, we heard Sammy Davis Jr. sing out: "Ding Dong! The Witch Is Dead!" from *The Wizard of Oz*. That's my father's wicked sense of humor to a T.

❦

OUR LOVED ones are always looking for new ways to communicate. Often they will turn our attention to something nearby that might have meaning for them or us, or that grabs our attention in an unusual way. We help them when we acknowledge their efforts. All we have to do is look up and smile. They love it when we say, "I know that's you!"

ALAN, THE young man who wanted to know as much as he could about the spiritual plane before he passed from liver cancer, and who channeled in the phrase *Love is greater than pain*, is a big Bob Marley fan. As he was preparing for his transition, he often listened to Marley's music. The song "Three Little Birds" spoke to all of us, especially when we heard the part that Alan liked to emphasize, "Don't worry about a thing, 'cause every little thing's going to be alright."

After Alan's passing, his family and friends gathered at the cemetery for his funeral. Suddenly, we heard a woman's voice, loud and clear, singing, "Don't worry about a thing, 'cause every little thing's going to be alright!"

We were stunned into silence. We looked to see where the voice was coming from. A woman, atop a big brown horse, was riding through the cemetery and singing away! When she saw us and realized that there was a funeral about to start, she came closer and apologized. She explained that she'd experienced a sudden and urgent need to sing that song! We realized that Alan, always a true romantic, had arranged this, down to the beautiful image of a lovely lady on a horse.

How did Alan do this? When I asked him, through channeling, he told me he just started singing that song in her ear and she felt compelled to chime in.

Alan reports that he loved his family's and friends' responses to the song. How could we keep from smiling when we knew that Alan was playing with us, trying to ease our pain? This is another example of how I know that love endures on both sides!

Fay, Alan's mom, had confided to me that she had set aside money to someday put toward her son's wedding. Instead, she threw a celebration of Alan's life, honoring his reunion with Divine Consciousness on the spiritual plane. Three hundred and fifty people showed up, double the number expected. After several people spoke of Alan's many attributes, I had the honor of channeling him so he could directly address his loved ones. But when I stood at the podium looking out at the crowd, Alan was silent! I could feel him standing next to me. When I looked at him, I saw his spiritual manifestation, as he channeled to me that he was overwhelmed by the outpouring of love. After looking back at the expectant crowd, I turned once again to Alan—thank God we were communicating telepathically! "Oh [expletive]," I told him, "Alan, say something!" Alan did a double take, laughed his contagious laugh, and then channeled what he wished to share with his loved ones.

Several months later, Fay asked me to accompany her to a gathering of Compassionate Friends, the support group for bereaved parents. Walking from the car to the meeting, we passed a hair salon. Blaring from behind its locked doors, we heard Bob Marley's voice, singing, "Don't worry about a thing . . ." Fay and I just stopped and listened. We could feel Alan with us.

OUR LOVED ones are always looking for ways to communicate. Their methods are as diverse and creative as they are themselves.

Todd: Paradise

Todd's parents were devastated when they got the call. Todd, forty-one years old, had passed in his sleep after suffering for years from debilitating back pain, diabetes, and heart trouble. A couple of weeks after he passed, they received a phone call from a number they did not recognize. They let the call go to their answering machine. After the beep, they heard music and lyrics in another language. A hoarse whisper said, "Hello. How are you?" and then the line disconnected. After listening several times, Todd's parents fed the song's lyrics into the computer. The translation was "I am not in pain." They then called the number back. A woman answered with one word: "Paradise." Todd's mom and dad were dumbfounded. It turned out that the call had come from a nursing facility with the word "Paradise" in its name. When Todd's father told the woman who answered the phone about the call they had received, she replied that she found that impossible. There had been no outgoing calls on that line all day. It seems to me that Todd must have done quite a bit of work to make sure his parents knew he was in "Paradise."

Todd wants to add that he had ongoing mental health and addiction issues during much of his life. As a result, he felt an intense need to let his parents know that he was allowed into Paradise in spite of his troubled past.

Todd's mom, Susan, often finds what she refers to as "pennies from heaven." She knows that when she finds one, it is Todd's way of saying hello. Recently, while I was channeling Todd, he told his mom that he would up the ante. She started finding nickels and dimes! She found them in unlikely places, often at home where she knew that people were not just dropping them. Todd loves his mom's reaction and says that he's working his way up to twenties! Susan just let me know that she found a five-dollar bill.

Birds and Butterflies

Ryan's soccer team number was 17. He was born on the seventeenth of the month and always considered it to be his number. When Ryan was sixteen, he passed in a car accident on the seventeenth of the month.

Ryan will often draw his family to the number 17. It's his way of telling them that he is with them. Ryan's mom, Carol, and I met at a restaurant and, sitting at an outside table, I channeled Ryan. Then Carol shared stories of his childhood. As we sat, little birds started to gather on the empty chair next to us. There was no food to entice them, as our plates had long been cleared away, but it seemed that their arrival was quite deliberate. So many had gathered. We counted them and then counted again. Seventeen!

Like Troy, who brought his father an owl, our loved ones can direct birds and butterflies to come close to us. They can also direct us to focus our energy so we will see their efforts. They report through channeling that they are not taking over or possessing the bird or butterfly, just tapping into the energy and guiding a beautiful resource to us as a sign.

As I write this, I'm being told to tell you that they are pretty creative in interacting with willing creatures. Depending on your location and climate, you might have a sign through a lizard, deer, or dragonfly. Hummingbirds are a favorite, if available, not just for their beauty, but also for their high vibration, as the higher the vibration, the easier for the out-of-body loved one to communicate with the bird and us. One out-of-body young man wants to share that because his family lives in the city, he often enlists the help of pigeons and an occasional squirrel.

How do we know when we are receiving an intentional communication? These signs are often brought to us when we need them most. They may occur when we are thinking of our loved ones, enjoying a fond memory, or wondering what they would say if they knew what we were doing—or our loved ones may simply be responding to our heart's needs. I believe we instinctively "know" when it's the real deal, maybe because the experience comes with a little energetic hug. During a channeling session, if the out-of-body person describes the signs they have been sending, invariably the in-body person receiving the information exclaims, "I knew it!"

When we acknowledge and appreciate their efforts, they are comforted, much like we are. Our open recognition helps them as they help us.

Celia: "For the first time, I'm not worried about him."

Every year or so, a healer by the name of Romy would make the rounds in Southern California. A client friend would let me know when he was coming to town and, until now, I had always declined, not feeling the need to see him.

The summer of 2009 was different. When my friend told me of Romy's upcoming visit, she added that he would be working near my home. As I was about to politely pass on this opportunity, I heard an out-of-body male voice saying, "Please go!" I heeded the instruction. When I arrived at the host's home, I found a room full of people waiting to see Romy. I immediately noticed a beautiful woman, a bit older than I am, who I thought resembled my mother. My eyes were drawn right above her head to a handsome out-of-body young man.

"I'm the one who asked you to come! Can you please tell my mom that I'm okay?"

I walked over to the woman and quietly told her that there was a very persuasive young man hovering right above her claiming to be her son. He wanted to reassure her that he was doing fine. Her eyes got big and then welled up as she explained, "My son, Jack, was killed by a train while he was riding his bike, less than six months ago, on December twenty-third." I looked up and caught her son's eye as I told her that he'd passed on my birthday.

Jack had me tell his mother that he didn't suffer; in fact, he didn't even realize that he had left his physical body. The first person he saw on the other side was his aunt Carlotta.

JACK: She held out her hand to help me, and I thought, "Oh shit! I must be dead!"

His mother laughed. "Yup, that's Jack all right!"

CELIA, WHO would go on to become one of my dearest friends, confided that she had just that morning begged God for a sign that her son was with her. I then learned that Celia was the person who was hosting Romy. We both laughed at how Romy's visit set the ball in motion, but it was Jack who'd arranged the healing.

Jack launched right in and was more than eager to share the details of his life and passing with his mom. He had been schizophrenic and wanted to thank her for never giving up on him. The path wasn't easy and was sometimes dramatic, but Celia was always there to guide and love her son. At the time of the accident, the difficulty was easing and life was going well.

Over the course of my friendship with Celia, Jack would often pop in to talk to his mom. Celia, already extremely intuitive, was now having her own visions and visits with Jack.

Having had a life review, Jack now understood why he'd suffered through such mental anguish and upheaval. One reason was to experience unconditional love in spite of his behavior. This, his mother had provided.

One day, while we were channeling Jack, Celia started to cry. "I'm crying with relief!" she said. "For the first time, I don't have to worry about him! He's not suffering or in pain. He's not lost, he's not hungry!"

I was floored by Celia's observation. She was allowing her love— her need for her son's well-being—to be greater than her pain.

Jack says that his mother's well-being is everything to him. He is comforted knowing that Celia, while still missing him on the physical plane, is not in anguish worrying about him. This frees him up to create some fun-loving and healing mischief.

Jack's and Celia's concerns are reciprocal. They are able to reassure each other. Jack, no longer in his physical body, does not have any mental health affliction and is growing, learning, and enjoying manifesting playful communication.

I'm impressed with Jack's tenacity and grateful that he brought our families together. When I spend time with his mom, he will sometimes channel in a comment about what we're doing, or about what he is doing. He loves when he can point out a correlation. Even though I don't remember the details of what I channel, I am aware of and appreciate Jack's consistent sweetness and humor, partly because—and I love this part—he comes in to hug me once in a while! He says it's okay to share that.

Jack: "I love to watch my mother dance!"

A few years later, on Jack's birthday, I called Celia and asked if she would like to go out for breakfast. She said yes and I proceeded to follow Jack's instructions. I put together a little gift. I was told to wrap it in vibrant pink and green.

JACK: The perfect ribbon is in the back of your kitchen drawer!

I opened the drawer, the one that accumulates odds and ends, and found a velvet avocado ribbon I had shoved in weeks earlier.

JACK: Not that one. Check way in back.

There I found the perfect lime green ribbon that I hadn't known was in there! Jack laughed at my astonishment.

Usually when Celia and I go out, we each weigh in on our preferences. This time, I picked her up and didn't give her a choice. We went straight to a lovely café with outside seating adjacent to a large park-like plaza.

When I gave Celia the gift, she started to cry. The pink and green colors had particular significance, she told me. Also, it turned out that the scents of the aromatherapy healing gloves were her favorites. She held her hands up and asked how I knew that her hands had been hurting. I told her that I didn't know, but apparently Jack did. He directed my gift choice. Just then my phone buzzed. One of my children, who had no idea what was transpiring between Celia and me, had texted a picture of a beautiful tree, lime green, covered with vivid pink flowers.

After breakfast, I was instructed to tell Celia to go sit in the nearby plaza and that I would meet up with her shortly. She went and sat down and noticed that a dance floor was being set up. I joined her just in time to see two women in full flamenco dress step onto the dance floor. Music started and they were terrific! At the end of their dance, they came up to Celia, and only Celia, though she was one of many people sitting and watching, and asked her to come up and dance with them. They didn't know, as I did, that Celia had been a passionate professional flamenco dancer in her younger days. They also didn't know, and neither did I, that just that morning, Celia had been talking about how Jack, when he was young, had loved to watch his mother dance.

As I watched Celia dancing, I heard Jack loud and clear: "I got my birthday present! I got to watch my mother flamenco dance!" My jaw was hanging open and my eyes filled with tears as I marveled at his ingenuity. When the performance ended, I relayed Jack's message. Celia couldn't have been more delighted.

As the performers were packing up, we approached and asked if they performed here regularly. "Oh no" was the reply. "It's one time only—we've never done it here before." As Celia and I looked at each other in astonishment, I could hear Jack laughing.

Sam: Sometimes You Just Need Mom's Reassurance

Suzanne's husband passed after complications following a heart transplant. He was happy to relay to his wife, through channeling, how grateful he was for her love and care. He shared details of his life and the circumstances of his passing. Suzanne listened intently, agreeing with all that her husband said.

Suddenly, Suzanne interrupted him. "Where's my Sam?" she cried out! A blond young man presented himself. He was grinning from ear to ear while spinning a basketball on his finger.

SAM: I made Dad promise not to say anything. I needed you to ask for me! I just need to know I wasn't too much of a burden.

SUZANNE: What? When you went, all the fun went with you!

Sam was beaming. He was obviously extremely happy with his mother's response.

SAM: Mom! Look what I can do!

Sam shot some hoops and demonstrated his agility.

Suzanne was crying with joy and I could see her husband beaming.

I had no idea what all this was about, so I was eager to have Suzanne explain. Sam, in his physical life, had inhabited a body with a neurological disorder. He had no control over his muscles— he'd never walked, talked, or fed himself. Through channeling, he projected a picture of what he looked like during his physical life. It was a disconcerting sight, with his eyes appearing unfocused and saliva running from the corner of his mouth. But Suzanne told me that he knew how to laugh and his parents knew how to make him happy. He especially loved being wheeled to the park to watch the neighborhood kids play basketball. He also loved going to the store and vying for the attention of girls.

Suzanne said that she would often see other parents looking at them with pity. She would smile, knowing they just didn't understand how much love and pure joy they experienced as a family. I cried as I listened to her share how much she and her husband appreciated their life with Sam.

Usually, when I channel, I see the person as he or she appeared in their physical life. But Sam, other than showing his past physical self for identification, presented himself as he is now, as a fully functioning young man. Sam reports that he really is enjoying playing basketball out there. The image was not shown just to appease his mother. He tells us that he can manifest and pursue his passions in much the way we can.

With his father looking on, Sam thanked his mother and discussed how he felt about his physical life and what he has since learned. He reassured his mother that the love and laughter outweighed any frustration. When Suzanne's husband reminded her that Sam wanted his mother's reassurance that he had not been too much of a burden, she was more than happy to emphasize again her gratitude for having had Sam as a son.

◇∞◇

PLEASE TELL your out-of-body loved ones how much you love them. They love to hear it just as we do. We may be hurt and angry over their leaving the physical plane, or like Bob in Chapter 4, whose father rejected him, we may have lingering issues about things that transpired while they were here in body. Either way, we can address our issues with compassion and kindness, for ourselves as well as for them. When we do, we clear a space, and we open up to more than communication and healing with our loved ones. We also open ourselves up to fully embracing the physical world and the wonderful people and gifts it holds. Don't forget, releasing our burdens raises our vibrational frequency even further, increasing our joy and enhancing our ability to receive spiritual communication.

JACK WANTS me to share with you that his ongoing healing and interaction with his mom was what enabled him to do the networking needed to support the birthday shenanigans. Yes, Jack chose the word "shenanigans," because he says it fits him and his desire to make his mother laugh!

As for Sam, it seems he just needed to make sure that his mom didn't feel that his physical life was too big a burden. Suzanne reassured him that she wouldn't have traded even a moment that she had with him. She knows that his laughter is still ringing true and that his father can hear him loud and clear.

Laughter Is the Best Medicine

There is great wisdom in that phrase, especially when we are aware that laughter is a surefire way to raise our vibrational frequency. Our out-of-body loved ones know this and will often use humor to put their loved ones at ease, and help dispel any fear when we are about to channel.

We had just started the session and Darleen was excited to hear what would come in. I could see her father as he manifested directly over her head.

Me: Your dad is right here with you and it feels like he is the main person you are wanting to talk to.

Darleen: That's right.

Me: It's weird. He's right here, but he's not saying anything. He's not talking.

Darleen smiled and waited.

Me: I see him, but he keeps disappearing and then reappearing. I clearly get that he's your dad, but I don't understand why he hasn't said a word. And why he keeps doing the disappearing thing.

This went on for a couple of minutes more. I explained to Doreen that once in a while, it takes a little extra time to figure out what's going on, and the glitch generally makes sense once we do. At that point, Darleen could not contain her laughter.

Darleen: That's unbelievable! You just proved that it's really him. My dad was a deaf magician!

I could hear Darleen's dad laughing along with us. Her father then went on to talk to his daughter for a couple of hours without any hesitation.

A large family gathered for a session after the patriarch passed. Everyone was solemnly waiting for his words of wisdom.

"I don't have a leg to stand on! That's right, I don't have a leg to stand on!" he said when he appeared.

I could hear him laugh and soon realized that, starting with the teenage grandchildren, everyone was laughing. They laughed until they cried as they informed me that this was definitely Grandpa's sense of humor. It turned out that Grandpa had had a leg amputated a couple of months before his transition to the spiritual plane!

CLEARLY, WE take our personality with us. And beautifully, if we had a physical impairment, either from birth, or later in life, we no longer have it after we pass. This goes for mental impairment, if it is physically caused, as well. If our particular situation on this plane is a means through which to grow, only the learning curve is permanent. Out-of-body people will often discuss former physical challenges with us, revealing insights they have garnered since going out of body.

FROM THE time I was little, I always loved the comedian Totie Fields. She could find the humor in every situation, including health challenges. After losing a leg to diabetes and a breast to cancer, she quipped that God was looking to take her. But, she went on, she didn't want to go yet, so she and God had reached an agreement. God would take her in parts!

While I admired Totie's spunk, I realized that there was more to her humor than the obvious. To me, she was a brilliant negotiator, since her soul—the part of her that animates the vehicle—did not diminish one bit, even if some of her physical parts were gone.

CHAPTER 9

How Connecting
Helps Us and Our
Loved Ones

O ne of the best things we can do to multiply our joy and diminish our sorrow is to share our experiences with others who are going through similar circumstances. Support groups do more than introduce us to new friends or allow us to vent. The sharing of emotion tends to make us more empathic. As we allow ourselves to be more open, our compassion for others expands. The resulting vulnerability and authenticity raise our vibration. If the discussion takes a spiritual turn, the frequency of the group rises even higher. This is why so many bereaved people report receiving a sign or communication near the time of their support meetings.

As we know, whether we're fully conscious of it or not, when our vibration rises it is easier for our out-of-body loved ones to get through to us. We become more aware of and receptive to their efforts. So imagine if we all come together in a group while sharing the same intention, to honor and love those who have transitioned out of body. The camaraderie, that feeling of not being isolated or alone while experiencing overwhelming grief, further raises the vibrational frequency. This healing energy then gives fuel to those on the spiritual plane. There's so much more going on than meets the eye. For example, when Alan's mother, Fay, and I attended a meeting of Compassionate Friends, the support group for bereaved parents, I saw a room filled with out-of-body children who had accompanied their parents to the meeting. As the parents offered each other support, their children met, some for the first time, and did the same. They shared tips on how to help their parents and siblings find joy in the physical world. They were all trying to get through to comfort their parents and let them know they were still with them.

Yes, they network out there and try to help us.

As we know, Alan managed to bring us his favorite Bob Marley tune as his mom and I were going to the Compassionate Friends meeting. That song was just the beginning of his networking efforts to help Fay, and other parents as well.

The meeting began with everyone in a circle introducing themselves and sharing the circumstances that had brought them to the group. After Fay told the group about Alan, I introduced myself and shared that I loved Alan and his family and was there to support Fay. Maybe it was the perceptive meeting facilitator, but to my surprise I soon found myself sharing the pain and grief I'd felt over the miscarriage I'd had many years earlier. I really didn't feel that my loss had any significance in relation to the suffering of this brave group of parents, but the kind lady running the meeting thought otherwise. Though it had happened more than thirty years earlier, I was flooded with memories. Back then, I was unable to find any books focusing on this kind of loss. Harry, who was working at a prominent children's hospital at the time, was told that his situation did not merit even one day off to heal and grieve. Luckily the miscarriage had occurred on a weekend. Though we had family and close friends with whom to share our devastating news, we didn't know how to move forward or deal with the depression.

Love and support came in a way we'd least expected. Several women, including my mother-in-law, shared the untold stories of their own miscarriages. These conversations were held in private and in hushed tones, as if there was shame in experiencing such a loss. I realized that these women had kept their grief to themselves. There just wasn't a convenient place to process it. Like in the days of old, when women shared their woes at the well, the camaraderie of these ladies helped give me strength. Thankfully, acknowledgment and recognition of the need for healing from this kind of loss is more available these days.

After our initial sharing at the Compassionate Friends meeting, we were separated into three groups for deeper discussions. Each group settled into its own room. I listened while Fay and others in our group talked about their children. I could see and hear these children as they hugged their parents and encouraged them to continue speaking.

Suddenly, a couple entered the room, both looking a bit bewildered. The woman apologized and said they were supposed to be in a different group, but she'd had this overwhelming impulse that she needed to be with us. Her husband, though not understanding the compulsion, had accompanied her. With them was their son, a handsome out-of-body young man, who looked at me and said, "Tell them! Tell them I'm here!"

I wasn't sure how to proceed, but at that moment I saw Fay's son, Alan, joking and talking with this new couple's son. I waited for the end of this portion of the meeting, when we took a break and were invited to socialize. I approached the couple and told them that their son was standing with them, surrounded by three golden retrievers. I had their full attention, as they informed me that the family had had three golden retrievers when their son was younger.

This was how I met Todd, who, we later learned through his phone call to his parents, is in Paradise. Alan reveals that he helped Todd persuade his parents to leave their group and join ours. Alan had told Todd that if he brought them over, I would be able to channel him for his parents, and this was something that Todd desperately wanted, since he wanted them to know he was no longer in pain. He told his dad, a medical doctor, the details of the maladies he'd had while in body. The facts were indisputable as Todd welcomed his parents into the reality that he was with them and happy to communicate. And, through it all, Alan stood by, giving support to his new friend.

I am blessed in that I, along with my family, have become friends with everyone involved. Todd and Alan will often show up together. They remind me as I write this that we all made new friends that day.

∽∞⌀

DON'T FORGET, your loved ones are with you and love to be talked about and celebrated. While you're doing that, they are not only listening, they are socializing with each other, enjoying each other's company, and cooking up new ways to reach you.

OUR OUT-OF-BODY loved ones can be very persuasive and creative in their efforts to facilitate healing in every direction. While they want us to embrace each other and continue to thrive on the physical plane, they share that they are doing the same on the spiritual plane.

Remember Ryan, who brought his mother, Carol, seventeen birds? He continually lets his family know that he is involved and knows what is going on in their lives. He likes to actively keep his family aware of what he has been up to, as well. He encourages his family to continue being involved with Compassionate Friends and is proud of his father's acknowledgment, during a speech that he gave, that "our children are with us." Ryan goes along with his parents to the meetings to help all the parents and other out-of-body kids. Like his parents, he finds that he really enjoys socializing and meeting new people. He particularly hit it off with an out-of-body young lady he had never met during his physical life. Like Ryan, she accompanied her parents to the meeting. As their relationship developed, Ryan had a desire that is typical for those in body. He wanted his mom to meet this young woman's mother.

During a channeled session, Ryan told Carol all about his new friend. He described what she had looked like on the physical plane and the circumstances of her transition out of body. As he shared, he became more animated, eventually blurting out, "Wait a minute, I'm going to figure out a way for you to meet her mom. You'll see! You're going to meet this lady and realize that it's my friend's mother. I'll find a way."

A couple of weeks later, I received a call from Carol. "It happened! Ryan did it! It was the craziest thing."

Carol had gone to the cemetery and was deep in thought when she spotted a woman close by who appeared to be lost. Carol approached and asked if she could help her. The woman was puzzled.

She had come to visit her daughter's grave, as she often does, but had become disoriented. This had never happened before and she had wandered quite a way and was unfamiliar with this part of the cemetery. Carol's heart jumped. Could this be the mom that Ryan wanted her to meet? She asked about the woman's daughter as she helped the woman find her bearings. She tried to hide her astonishment as she was told, in much the same words that Ryan had used, of how the daughter had passed. Just as Carol was about to ask if this mother's child had long blond hair and blue eyes, the mom took out a photograph. There she was! The young woman her son had described! Though she didn't feel it appropriate to share all that she knew, she could sense Ryan and his elation that he had accomplished what he'd set out to do.

NETWORKING HAPPENS in creative ways. We might not be aware of how pervasive it is, but when we can connect the dots, it is astounding!

Chris

Eighteen years ago, I channeled Chris for his large extended family. He was sixteen and had fallen asleep at the wheel on his drive home. He assured everyone that his transition was quick and painless. In fact, he didn't immediately realize that he had transitioned. It wasn't until he turned and saw his grandfather, who had come to greet him, that he understood what had happened.

Chris had messages for everyone present, and for his father, who was too overcome with grief to attend the session. The family was reassured and delighted to find that he was still the thoughtful and considerate Chris they knew.

Several years later and a thousand miles away, when I channeled a young man, Steve, for his mom, I was caught by surprise. I could see Chris standing right behind him! After Steve told his mother about the circumstances of his passing, which were similar to Chris's, I asked Chris about his connection and why he was showing up in this session.

Chris said he was running a support group for young guys who had passed in the same manner as he had. He knew firsthand the guilt and surprise that often accompanies this type of passing and wanted to help others acclimate to the sudden change in circumstances. Steve, whose passing was somewhat recent, felt so guilty and distraught by his parents' grief that Chris, his support group leader, had promised to help him find a way to communicate with his mother.

I then asked Steve's mom how she had come to know of me. She said it was very strange. While she was in a doctor's waiting room, the receptionist approached her. She apologized for the intrusion and said she had a strong impulse to give her my card. She told Steve's mom about her nephew and how channeling had helped the family. The receptionist was Chris's aunt!

As I write this, Chris and Steve are right here saying that this is just the tip of the iceberg. There is more networking happening out there than we can imagine. It is extensive and our out-of-body loved ones are delighted when we acknowledge their efforts.

Please Let Me Help

Andrea and Rick had been married for twenty-two years. Though Rick was quite a few years older than Andrea, she was still shocked to come home and find that he had passed from a heart attack while puttering about in the garden.

Rick always knew that he was emotionally reserved. But while studying his life review, he was blindsided by what appeared to be his cold withdrawal. He saw, as he examined their life together, that his wife continually pleaded for more emotional intimacy. While in body, he chalked up his aloofness to being the result of trauma he sustained while fighting in the Vietnam War. Rick's dismay that he came across as willfully withholding during his adult years is indicative of his true good nature and compassionate heart. He revealed, through channeling, that he'd never intended to hurt his wife. During their marriage Andrea had tried to explain her emotional needs. Rick had not been responsive. Now that he was out of body and could clearly see his inadvertent contribution to perpetuating the problem, he was horrified. He received loving guidance to help him understand cause and effect. His pain was so deep and repressed that he had subconsciously kept almost all emotion at bay, lest it open the floodgates and overpower him.

It is not surprising to learn that Rick is a compassionate dog lover. During his life review, this was pointed out to him. He was a softie when it came to his canine pals. This empathy provided an outlet for the sweetness he worked so hard, unknowingly, to suppress.

RICK: I can't believe how cold I was. That was never my intention. I feel so stupid. Andrea, you kept trying. You even threatened to leave. Why didn't you? I see now how lonely you were. I'm so mad at myself for not being able to understand what was right in front of me. I realize now that you gave up and stopped trying a lot of years ago. I never meant to cause you pain, but I obviously did. I'm so angry at myself.

ANDREA: Wow! This is definitely you. That's how it was. I knew you weren't doing it on purpose. I got that part. I used to ask myself why I stayed. The bottom line was that I love you, and I knew that underneath it all, you loved me, too. I saw that you couldn't express it, but you always wanted to take such good care of me. I realized that you show your love that way. And I felt bad for you.

RICK: But you were the one suffering, because of me.

ANDREA: Rick, you weren't trying to hurt me, I know you weren't that way on purpose. Please don't be mad at yourself. I understand

RICK: I love you! I do!

ANDREA: I know. I love you, too.

RICK: I'm so sorry.

Rick went on to talk about the things he'd worked so hard to suppress after his war years. During his physical life, he did not believe in anything spiritual. He thought that when you died, that was the end of it. He admitted that while he was in body, he had hoped this was true. At least there wouldn't be retribution or an angry God to contend with.

RICK: It's unbelievable! It's all about love out here. Andrea, those two guys who were my friends, who died right in front of me in the war, they came right up and hugged me. I hated myself because I couldn't help them. They died, and not me. They hugged me! Can you believe that? They told me that they felt bad for me all these years. They felt bad for me! They could see, and I see now, too, that I was never the same after they died. Andrea, you suffered because of this, and that makes me so angry at myself.

ANDREA: No, no, let it go! Don't be angry at yourself, I understand.

RICK: I know, I know. They keep telling me that out here, too. You know what I realize now? That I was starving myself emotionally, not just you. It was like a piece of myself forgot how to be a person. They help you here. I can see now that how I was behaving doesn't fit with who I truly am.

ANDREA: Maybe I felt that and that's why I always still loved you, even when I was angry.

RICK: Andrea, I get it, I do. But here's the thing: I shut myself out, not just you. I blocked my own self!

ANDREA: I realize that.

RICK: Oh, Andrea, I'm so sorry that I can't come back and make it up to you. I probably wouldn't know how to do that anyway. So, here's what we're going to do. I'm going to search and find a good man who is not afraid. I want you to have what you always wanted. I want you to talk and travel and really have fun. Will you let me do that? Are you open to that?

ANDREA: Yes, I would like that. I would like to meet someone I can talk to. I'd like someone who will talk to me.

RICK: Okay! I'm on the job.

ANDREA: But, Rick, you have to know that I do love you. I really do.

RICK: I really love you, too. That's why I want you to have everything. Just because I couldn't do it doesn't mean you should go without.

A FEW weeks later, Andrea decided to heed her friend's advice and look into going to a bereavement support group meeting. She had a list of days and times for the different groups in her area. On the day she planned to go, she had a sudden urge to not go to the meeting in her own town, but to attend a meeting a couple of towns away. She followed her instincts. At that meeting she met a man who had recently taken care of his wife, as she had gone through, and passed from cancer. They found it incredibly easy to talk to each other, share their stories, and more. Andrea had a feeling that Rick was behind her decision to go to that fortuitous meeting. She set up another channeling session with me to find out and brought her new friend, Walter, with her.

WHEN ANDREA and Walter sat down together in front of me, I immediately saw Rick right above Andrea's head. Over Walter's head, I saw a woman and correctly assumed that she was his wife who had passed.

RICK (BEAMING WITH HAPPINESS): I told you! I'm so happy for both of you.
ANDREA: So you set this up?
RICK: I had a little help.
[I saw the woman move in closer.]
RICK: We had a collaboration.

. . .

WALTER'S WIFE channeled in to thank him for taking such good care of her during her illness. She confided that she, too, after she passed, was looking for someone who would be a good fit for Walter. In her own out-of-body support group, she had met Rick. They realized pretty quickly that the spouses they'd left behind on the physical plane would be a good match.

ANDREA: So you set it up! I knew it, Rick, I knew it had to be your influence. I'm not impulsive that way. I knew you had a hand in getting me to go to that particular meeting!

Andrea and Walter are now engaged.

∞

I'VE CHANNELED in, time and time again, a loving spouse planning and arranging romantic and synchronistic meetings for the loved one left on the physical plane. They report that when a person really loves someone, they will do whatever they can to try to make them happy. They seem to be pretty successful in their efforts.

CLEARLY, LOVE is not just greater than pain. It's bigger than any possible jealousy as well. People often want to know what will happen if they have a loving partner who has passed, in addition to a new love relationship on the physical plane. Through channeling, we learn that out-of-body partners will not just be matchmakers for those they love on the physical plane, they are also grateful to the in-body new partners for bringing happiness to the ones they love. Not only is there no jealousy, the out-of-body partners will often hug and thank the newer in-body partners upon their return to the spiritual plane. It is not unusual for all involved to be in the same soul group.

Guides channel in an analogy. When you light a candle, the flame brings warmth and light. If you light another candle next to the first one, of course the warmth and light are amplified. Now look back at the first candle. Has the flame diminished? Of course not. Your loyalty and love for one who has passed is not undermined or diminished if, and when, new love comes along. Of course, this analogy is true of all types of relationships. Love for a child who has passed is not diminished by loving a new baby or the children who are still on the physical plane. Likewise, expanding or new friendships on the physical plane do not diminish the love for a friend who has passed.

People who are out of body may fall in love with each other as well. But the people who have channeled in the desire to find a partner for the one they left behind on the physical plane report that they have little desire to do the same for themselves. They tell us that those in the physical body have more of a physical yearning to have contact and companionship, and because they know their partner so well, they like to offer their help to facilitate an appropriate match.

I HAVE come to realize that out-of-body networking may take tenacity, requiring several steps to reach us and make the connection.

Dad: I'll Find a Way to Talk to My Son

I would often channel for a friend who is a casting director. One evening, while we were chatting, her mom channeled in and mentioned the specific type of actor her daughter was casting for a project she was currently working on.

My friend: That's right, we're testing for the male lead tomorrow!

Mom: The right guy is coming in tomorrow. He's perfect and will get the part.

Bryan had come to this country from Australia with the desire to become a movie actor. He had never acted before and had no formal training, but this did not stop him from pursuing his dream. He had apparently come to the attention of my friend's mom, who channeled in a detailed description of him, so that her daughter would be sure to recognize him.

The following evening, I talked to my friend. She informed me that an actor, Bryan, had come in to audition. He fit her mother's description perfectly but did not get the part. My friend's mom immediately channeled in her reply.

Mom: Don't worry. He's the right guy! You're going to "discover" him with this part you're casting. He's going to be a big movie star!

The next day, my friend requested that they bring Bryan back for another audition. The team making the movie was not interested. My friend persisted. She was so sure of Bryan's potential, she told them, that if they brought him back in, hired him, and were not happy with the results, she would return her casting fee. They acquiesced. Bryan was brought back in for another audition. My friend's mom had already channeled in her instructions.

Mom: He was trying too hard the first time. This time, right before he starts his audition, go up to him and tell him to "play it from the heart." If you do this right before he opens his mouth, he won't have time to think too hard. He'll go right to playing it from the heart, which is exactly what they are looking for.

My friend followed her mother's instructions and Bryan got the part.

Not long after, I was visiting my friend at her office. On her desk was a vase of magnificent flowers. My friend showed me the card that had arrived with the bouquet:

"I'll always remember to play it from the heart."

My friend decided that we should tell Bryan what had transpired—where the instruction had come from. She picked up the phone right then and called him. When she described what had happened, he thought the whole thing was pretty intriguing. He asked to talk to me, and I took the phone and shared all that I had perceived.

A few weeks later, at the end of the rehearsal period and before the start of filming, Bryan's manager threw a party for him. Bryan invited my husband and me to the celebration.

As my husband drove us up to Los Angeles, I could hear and see in my mind's eye that someone wanted very strongly to channel in. Bryan's dad presented himself.

BRYAN'S DAD: Thank you for helping my son! Yes, it's very exciting, and yes, I believe he will be a big movie star. That's all wonderful, but the thing is, I really want to get a message to him.

ME: Okay, but will I have the opportunity to tell him? It's a party!

BRYAN'S DAD: We'll find a way. I'll show you.

The party was in full swing when we arrived. Bryan arrived a bit after us. We found him to be sweet, humble, and charming. Bryan hugged us and proceeded to tell everyone how he had come to get the part. The managers, agents, and casting directors who heard the story asked if I could channel for their work situations, too. I explained that while I have fun channeling for friends, my main purpose is to be a catalyst for healing. Much to my relief, the actor's father channeled in and gave me direction.

ME: Let's say Bryan's dad wanted to come through and say . . .

BRYAN'S DAD then supplied the personal words that would grab Bryan's attention and prove to him that his father was truly present. I could feel Bryan's dad's relief as Bryan pulled me to a quiet corner. There, his dad thanked him and shared what he wanted his son to know. The healing happened.

Bryan did go on to be a major movie star! I don't know how my friend's mother knew that this would happen, though I believe her impact was a contributing factor. The original direction to play it from the heart was the result of his father's networking. Bryan's father tells me that he knew his son was going to go to the audition, so he scouted out the situation. Out-of-body people who want to get a message across to a loved one on the physical plane can be pretty adept at finding someone who can accommodate their need. My friend's mom reports that she became aware of the father's plight and offered to help after meeting Bryan's father, which took place before Bryan even came in for his first audition. The father introduced himself to my friend's mother and shared that he wanted to thank his son for his love and compassion, given at a time when the father did not feel deserving of it. Though they did not previously know each other, they had something in common. Both were wanting to help their children on the physical plane. They hatched what my friend's mother refers to as the "perfect plan." Asking Bryan to play it from the heart connected him to his authenticity and ultimately brought the recognition that his father felt he deserved. His father tells me that he loves the fact that his son's big break came as the result of his tender heart, the exact thing he wanted to channel in to acknowledge.

This seemingly convoluted scenario helped both the casting director, who is credited with "discovering" new talent, and the actor who went on to a successful career. The scheme also paved the way for me to channel Bryan's father directly to his son. While I think it's wonderful that Bryan became a "star," I am even more impressed with the creative out-of-body networking that took place to "align the stars," allowing gratitude and love to flow from the spiritual plane to the physical plane.

Where there's a will, there's a way!

∞

CLEARLY, OUT-OF-BODY loved ones continue to support and enjoy their in-body loved one's growth. At our children's school performances, I could always recognize if a child had an out-of-body parent. Whether a child was reciting, singing, playing an instrument, or presenting a project, I could actually see the parent right up there with them. After my father passed, whenever my brother, Mark, played music I could see him right above Mark's head, enjoying the music he'd always loved. Now that our mother is out there, too, I see both parents at all of his performances.

YET I have come to realize that this type of family support is fairly basic. Out-of-body people go to much greater effort, reaching out and networking to mentor and support people they did not know on the physical plane. They do this simply because they share the same interests and passions. Over the years, I have received excellent medical care for various issues. When discerning whether a doctor is a proper fit, I will take note of his or her bedside manner and credentials. But I'll also look around for any out-of-body guides who may be assisting. I have learned from experience that well-intentioned practitioners, whether practicing traditional Western medicine, integrative medicine, or alternative modalities, will often have out-of-body support and assistance. Sometimes it may be a parent or grandparent, but usually it's an out-of-body person who studied and practiced medicine and passionately wants to continue contributing their expertise to the physical world. I will often discreetly acknowledge these out-of-body helpers and feel out whether their energy feels compatible with my particular needs. I can usually affirm the high vibrational level and purity of intention by feeling the "wave," an energetic positive-feeling hug.

Occasionally friends ask me to come to their doctors' appointments to check out the out-of-body medical assistants. I'm happy to do this, but I always point out that most people are already instinctively able to perceive, energetically, if a doctor, or his or her suggested medical advice, resonates with their needs. It may be a hunch, a wave of confidence, goosebumps, a warm fuzzy feeling, or just the opposite, the urge to hightail it out of there. Pay attention. Your gut instinct always wants to add its two cents, and in many cases those two cents are priceless. If you are not feeling clear about your intuition, you might ask an out-of-body loved one to weigh in. There are both subtle and not-so-subtle ways that your loved one will get their message across. They are always here to help you, especially when you are feeling vulnerable. Don't worry about bothering them. I constantly channel in that they love to help.

It is interesting to note that I will usually be advised by the out-of-body helpers whether or not it would be appropriate to acknowledge their presence to the in-body practitioner. Invariably, if I see the energy field of the in-body person move toward or merge with the energy of the out-of-body helper, it is safe to assume that the person in-body has some awareness of the collaboration. These are the people I will sometimes share my perception with, usually to learn that other patients have done the same and that the affirmation is appreciated.

WHAT A beautiful thing it is to know that everything we have learned is not wasted. We take our passion and expertise with us when we transition to the spiritual plane. How glorious it is to realize that the love and care we receive here on the physical plane is expanded there beyond what we can physically comprehend. The human experience continues, and we are not just allowed but encouraged, after we pass, to pursue our dreams, expand our consciousness, and continue to contribute to the well-being of the world.

Remember Matteo, from Chapter 5, who had a passion for learning about surgery? Though he didn't have the opportunity to become a doctor, he took his passion for medicine with him when he passed at age fourteen. He reports to his mother, through channeling, that he is actively assisting and learning how to help people who are suffering from the disease that took him out of his physical body.

I HAVE come to believe that we have out-of-body assistants for the arts, sciences, and just about any expansive, vibration-raising or healing activity we can come up with. While channeling for people who are passionate in their fields, I have had the honor of meeting some of the experts who have passed. Though I would not know most by sight or name, some are recognizable to me, and will share their background.

I'm sure my perception of this phenomenon is just a small indication of the tremendous networking that is going on out there. My assumption is that we all are receiving encouragement and support from experts, either known or unknown to us.

Here are some examples.

Louise Hay, the motivational author and the founder of the publishing company Hay House, who passed in 2017, has contributed so much to healing with her writing on the mind and body connection. She loves to channel in to advise and chat with the people she has worked with while in body. Occasionally, she pops in during my channeling sessions to advise and help those she was not connected to during her physical lifetime.

Wayne Dyer, the self-help author and motivational speaker who passed in 2015, has gotten into the habit of saying hello to his former editor. That was not really a surprise, as she is now both my friend and literary agent, and I enjoy channeling for her. The unexpected and much appreciated part came when he began to visit me when his friend was not present. Wayne and I had never met on the physical plane, but that hasn't stopped him from offering me his wise counsel.

Dizzy Gillespie has shown up in several of my channeling sessions to continue the collaboration with a musician he mentored during his time in his physical body. Other out-of-body musicians have weighed in with their advice and talent during our sessions, too.

Erma Bombeck, the clever and funny satirist, channeled in to a woman with whom she had no previous connection. Bombeck encouraged the woman to pursue her writing, telling her that she has an appealing and accessible style. The woman I was channeling for then confided that she was writing a book and loved Erma Bombeck's work.

Bobby Darin channeled in to encourage someone to continue to pursue a singing career. He told the man: "You have what it takes!" The person I was channeling for was astounded and shared that he once met Bobby Darin, sang for him, and received the same advice.

Lucille Ball

Years ago, I was invited to participate in a television show that one of the major networks was producing about clairvoyants. Two days were dedicated to putting mediums on tape as they channeled for a person they had never met. I arrived at the allotted time to be the last one on tape and was not present to hear any of the other channeled sessions.

As the microphone and lights were being adjusted, I started to download a message. Though I'd never met Lucille Ball on the physical plane, I have had several opportunities to channel her for someone who was a large part of her life. I did not know who I was channeling the first time, but was not surprised to discover it was Lucy, as she was a witty and exuberant communicator. Usually, if I'm channeling someone famous, I will not make the connection, which is just as well, since that awareness could be a distraction. But at the television studio, Lucy's fiery energy and humor were unmistakable, and at that point we were already well acquainted through channeling. Since my job on the show was to channel, I simply repeated what she told me to say.

ME: Before we start, there is someone here who would like to give you a message. Lucille Ball is present and would like you to know that "TV is the medium for the medium!"

Everything seemed to stop for a few seconds. I looked around at the stunned faces. I was a little surprised at the director's and TV crew's reactions. After all, the show was interviewing mediums, and I had expected laughter. In general, I found Lucy's opinions to be thoughtful and practical.

After the initial silence, everyone around me seemed to be talking at once. I later learned that I was not the first to channel Lucy's opinion. Several mediums, none of whom I knew, both earlier that day and the day before, had channeled the exact same message from her!

The people on the set were stunned, as they knew I had just arrived and did not have access to any of the other mediums' channeling.

Lucy was, and still is, advocating her belief that television is the medium for the medium. She likes that it is accessible and can be watched in the privacy of your own home. She, of all people, should know that television has the power to lift spirits and lighten heavy hearts. She has raised the vibrational frequency of countless people. Clearly, she loves humanity and wants to continue to bring us joy.

SEVERAL YEARS ago, I had the opportunity to channel for a well-known actress. Her husband, a funny, witty, and colorful character, came through and reminisced about some of the capers they'd shared with their friends in days gone by. A lot of these friends had already passed, and they came forward and channeled in their greetings. The husband went on to talk about more personal matters, eventually discussing the debilitating illness that had led to his transition. He reported that while the progression of his sickness had been devastating for both of them, the transition itself was easy. His wife was delighted and relieved to hear what he had to say.

At the end of our session, the actress asked if I knew who her husband was. I did not. She told me his name, and I started to cry as I told her that her husband was one of my favorite actors. I'd had no idea that he had passed! I would have recognized him if I'd seen him in body, but my brain did not make the connection, as often happens with well-known people. I believe I am occasionally blessed with this type of amnesia, as I was the first time I channeled Lucille Ball for her loved one. I see the person, but it feels to me that a separate part of my brain is doing the channeling, blocking out any recognition. I could feel the husband hug me, a warm energetic wave, as his wife told me about the star-studded lineup of friends who had just channeled in. Before I could catch myself and censor my thoughts, I telepathically asked the husband if I could tell my mother, who was also a big fan, that I had met him. He hugged me again and said, "Yes, you can tell your mother."

After this session, a funny thing started to happen. At the end of every session in which I channeled a well-known person whom my mother was a fan of, I would hear, "And yes, you can tell your mother!" It had become some kind of inside joke out there! Now that she is on the spiritual plane, my mother herself may show up at the end of a session to tell the person I just channeled in how much she admires their talent.

EVERY HONEST effort to relieve pain and suffering, bring joy and healing, and raise the frequency of our own as well as the collective vibration, is recognized by Divine Consciousness. We are encouraged to explore our own personal ways of manifesting Divine Consciousness for our own growth and the expansion of all.

Albert Einstein

So how do these artists and scientists on the other side share their work? Yes, they are channeled in by mediums, but they tell me through channeling that they are also quite adept at downloading information to those who are aligned with them. The in-body recipients of their ideas most likely have no idea that they are being supported by those whom they most admire. After all, since we are on the physical plane to rediscover who we are, if our out-of-body pals gave us all the answers, it would defeat our purpose. But they can guide us and help us advance our work for our own, and the collective, highest good.

I started channeling Albert Einstein over twenty years ago, when he spontaneously showed up to help a doctor who was actively applying Einstein's theories. The doctor was creating a new device that could promote physical healing through a combination of light and laser energetic frequencies. I must admit that I was skeptical at first. Yes, all the information coming through to the doctor was accurate and well beyond my knowledge of the subject. But still, Einstein?

One night, Einstein showed up at home, when I was not actively channeling. Spontaneous visits are not unusual but are more often from personal family members or close friends. I was surprised and delighted to realize who my spiritual visitor was. By this time, I had channeled him often enough to recognize him, visually as well as by his high-vibrational energetic frequency.

He brought with him an out-of-body companion he introduced as his daughter. He then shared some personal information about their relationship. He ended his narration by stating that he and his daughter were enjoying each other's company and "making up for lost time." At this time, I knew absolutely nothing about Einstein's personal life. Though I certainly appreciated the visit, I was confused about why he had come until, shortly afterward, a book was published that corroborated everything he had said. *Einstein: His Life and Universe* by Walter Isaacson chronicles much of Einstein's personal family life. I believe that he had wanted to signal to me that it really was he who was appearing to me—and that I could trust the science that he was conveying.

Since then, Einstein has come through somewhat regularly, usually to people working in the field of physics. One scientist asked what Einstein thought about the Higgs boson. I ended up with pages of diagrams and observations, very little of which I had previously known. Einstein talked about the Big Bang theory, the sixteenth-century mystic Isaac Luria, and vibrational frequencies. According to an article in the *Los Angeles Times* by Karen Kaplan on October 8, 2013, "If you know one thing about the Higgs boson, it's probably that it's called the 'God particle.' The Higgs boson is the particle associated with the Higgs field, an energy field that transmits mass to the things that pass through it. Peter Higgs and François Englert theorized in 1964 that this is how things in the universe—stars, planets, even people—came to have mass." An article in *National Geographic* by Michael Greshko, August 29, 2018, explains, "For decades, physicists sought the Higgs boson: the theorized 'God particle' whose alter ego, a field pervading the entire universe, endows matter with mass. In 2012, scientists finally found the elusive particle, and now, they've gained crucial new insights by watching it break apart." It makes logical sense to me that Einstein finds a correlation between the Higgs boson and the Big Bang theory. Perhaps more intriguing is his making the connection to the mystic Kabbalist Isaac Luria. According to the *New World Encyclopedia*, "In Luria's system of creation and restoration, the Infinite compresses itself in order to make room for the creation." In other words, Luria's theory proposed the need for empty space, into which the Creator could create. Einstein channels in that Luria was referring to and understood the concept that is now known as the Higgs field, into which mass can be created. The correlation between this theory, which Luria came up with in the 1500s, and the Higgs boson is remarkable.

While I try to recall more of what Einstein channeled in at that time, he comes in as I write this now to say that he basically was focusing on expansion and contraction, and its place in physics and quantum healing.

Einstein had an opportunity to help me apply these concepts to my own healing when I was diagnosed with cancer. I had not started treatment yet, and my surgeon was not optimistic. I was meditating when Einstein popped in with a direction: "Go to the ocean." This was easy, as we now live in San Diego, very close to the water. I was preparing to do this when my phone buzzed. My friend Amean texted, "I will meet you at the ocean!" We had not had any contact that day and he did not know about the instruction I had received, at least not through traditional physical communication. But knowing Amean, I was not surprised. Since Amean lives a hundred miles away, I knew he would be joining me in the spiritual rather than the physical sense. Still, his text was a physical corroboration of Einstein's instruction.

When I stood by the water's edge, Einstein channeled in and told me to focus on the waves.

"Watch! Expansion, contraction. Expansion, contraction. Now focus on your breath. Expansion, contraction. Expansion, contraction. Your body is made up of cells. They are constantly expanding and contracting. Let your cellular structure expand along with your breath and the ocean's waves. In that expanded state, let the cancer cells go. Picture those cells going into light. When your body contracts along with the ocean and your breath, you will have healing."

I did as instructed, went home, and called Amean to share my experience. He laughed as he told me something I did not yet know. Einstein himself would often go to the ocean and focus on expansion and contraction, a concept that contributed to his discovering the theory of relativity.

Though I had been told that the cancer had already spread to the lymphatic system, later scans before surgery showed that it was no longer in the lymph nodes. I still followed the rigorous medical protocols while integrating natural and spiritual modalities into my treatment, but I have no doubt that "Dr." Einstein's compassionate direction contributed to my healing.

Humility Is the Key to Humanity

Einstein channels in that those on the spiritual plane are selective in choosing whom they will mentor on the physical plane. He says there is no shortage of brilliant minds capable of expanding on their work. Yet this, in itself, is not enough. Many Nazis during World War II had sufficient scientific knowledge but did not put their talents to good purpose. With that in mind, Einstein and others look for those scientists who have humility, honor mankind, and hold the intention to contribute to the highest good. Clearly, Einstein desires "high-frequency" purpose and will contribute to nothing less. He says that "humility is the key to humanity, and because of this humanity and love, we will survive."

Einstein channels in a fascinating concept. He says that while technology offers infinite ways to expand the mind, he and his cohorts are more concerned with expanding the heart.

Several years ago, Einstein channeled:

> Knowledge without compassion is unbalanced. One of the greatest scientific minds in the world is housed in a body that does not function normally. Because of his physical infirmity, those who learn from him integrate his teaching in a broader way. You see, when you are with him, the heart has an automatic empathic response. Compassion for his physical condition opens the heart. All of the information is filtered and absorbed through the receiver's reciprocity. The mind will then integrate compassion with the expansion of science, balancing the technology with humanity.

Einstein was clearly referring to Stephen Hawking, the great theoretical physicist, cosmologist, and author, who passed in 2018 at the age of seventy-six. He far outlived so many others who suffered from ALS, more commonly known as Lou Gehrig's disease. Was Hawking's tenacity bolstered by the out-of-body scientists who saw the importance of the heart-and-mind connection? Now that Hawking has passed to the spiritual plane, I have no doubt that he is moving about freely, collaborating joyfully on both planes with those he admires, and mentoring his in-body students.

CHAPTER 10

Helping Our Loved Ones Heal After They've Passed

O ur loved ones want us to live each day knowing that they are fine, that they're with us, and that their love for us never dies. As we know, they are available to help us in our healing in deep and personal ways, even as they work to heal themselves. But what happens when they themselves had trouble living their lives on Earth, as a result of their own mental or emotional imbalance?

We know that our loved ones who have passed have support in examining their lives through a life review. But sometimes more intense therapy is needed. While most people have good intentions, many of us have unconsciously perpetuated patterns of behavior or beliefs from generations before us. As our out-of-body loved ones watch their life review, they might be astounded by the occasional, or even constant, state of unconsciousness they experienced or chose during their physical lives.

They communicate, through channeling, the many ways that this separation from their highest self can manifest during the physical life. Sometimes I can taste alcohol while channeling. When the person who passed was an alcoholic, the physical aspect—the alcohol—is of course left behind. But the toxic patterns may still need to be examined. The recovering and newly transitioned soul has an opportunity, during life review, to understand the initial intention behind the need for alcohol. Was the intention to self-medicate physical or emotional pain? Was it to cover over and repress trauma? Was there a family pattern that felt inevitable? While we don't bring our physical toxicity with us into the spiritual plane, its cause and perceived need can still affect and repress the soul's vibration. This is especially true if our loved one passed with the burden of unresolved and unexamined issues.

As Maya Angelou said, "When you know better, you do better." Our loved ones' healing works in conjunction with our own. When we consciously expand and learn, our out-of-body loved ones are stimulated by that energy, and vice versa. This happens whether we are aware of it or not, but of course bringing it to consciousness accelerates the healing.

During their life review, our newly transitioned loved ones are given assistance, from guides as well as family members who have passed before them. Observing unconscious or negative behaviors usually results in shame and self-loathing. But Divine Consciousness is clever! At this point, the soul is shown the unknown and unremembered circumstances that led them to emotional repression and unhealthy behavior. This assistance not only puts together the puzzle pieces of the parts of ourselves that feel incongruous, it provides the empathy we so desperately need as we are put in a position of self-evaluation.

If, during a particularly challenging life review, the soul cannot see its way clear for its own salvation, the spiritual guides are patient. The soul has the option to stick its head in the sand, ostrich-style, and stubbornly refuse help. But Divine Consciousness continues to be clever and dangles a beautiful reward. Souls are instructed to be unwavering in trying to uncover the cause and understand the reasons for the behaviors they are not proud of. Why? They are shown a truth that many find surprising. If the soul is willing to understand why they acted the way they did, and then put together the connections between intention and learned behavior, the next step available to them is to help us!

The urge to help will usually provide the impetus and determination to examine the lives of even those souls who are immobilized by shame. Once they observe and understand the reasons for the behaviors they are not proud of and the ways they may have perpetuated them, they will do everything in their power to help us heal along with them.

Their Love for Us Is Greater Than Their Own Pain!

We come to understand, again, that we have the ability to help our out-of-body loved ones, as they learn that they have the ability to help us. Do they have to help us heal? What I hear channeled in over and over is: "No, we don't have to, but we want to because we love you."

Often, underneath the pride, ego, and fear, there is love, and lots of it. It is channeled in over and over again that out-of-body people wouldn't be happy if they couldn't love and help those they love. This is often followed by "Especially if I didn't do such a good job while I was there."

Jerry

Jerry was an alcoholic when he was in physical body. He grew up observing alcoholics in his family and assumed that drinking to excess was the normal thing to do. He was able to function at a high level with a responsible job. He didn't think much about it, but he was vaguely aware that he was drawn to drink whenever there was the potential for emotion to expose his pain. He didn't really want to know what the pain was about. He just needed it to go away.

When Jerry realized after he passed that his daughter was grieving not just his physical loss but also the loss of the potential to get to know and understand him, it was a revelation. It was in response to his daughter's pain, not his own, which he was used to suppressing, that he began to examine his emotional avoidance. Wanting to address and ease her suffering, Jerry agreed to the out-of-body counseling and emotional rehab that was offered to him. Love was greater than his own pain and shame, and he became conscious enough to want to examine and address his fears.

JERRY: Listen, we have the option to just stay in our own guilt and fear, but once you know you have options, it's pretty crazy to stay miserable. There are always people right here to help us. You can call them angels, guides, or whatever you want. Doesn't matter. They don't yell at you or try to make you feel bad. They help with cause and effect, and with examining the "why" behind our actions. We're encouraged to examine ourselves with compassion.

DAUGHTER: Dad, that's so wonderful. I'm really happy for you!

JERRY: Well, we're encouraged to learn about ourselves, not hide from ourselves.

DAUGHTER: That's just amazing!

JERRY (SHEEPISHLY): Just like on Earth! The irony is that help on Earth is a reflection of what's going on out here. There are people—doctors, therapists, and all kinds of angels on Earth—who are aligned to help. We just have to allow it! We really don't have to wait until our physical passing to figure things out. But since I did, I promise I'll keep working on it. I want you to live a good, long life, and when you get here, I want to be a dad you want to hug and be proud of. Meanwhile, I'll be here to watch over you. I already feel closer to you than I did when I was there in the physical. Maybe instead of losing your dad, you're starting to get your dad back!

FATHER AND daughter then expressed how much they love each other in spite of the challenges they had during their physical relationship.

⌘

ALCOHOL IS not the only device used to suppress emotion. People can hide their authenticity in many ways, employing patterns that are not only socially acceptable but applauded.

Maryanne

The colon cancer diagnosis was not a complete shock. Maryanne knew it ran in the family. She was fifty-three years old. Young enough, she thought, to power through treatment and get back to her busy life. She diligently followed medical protocol.

A natural leader, who was smart and empathic, Maryanne had the internal resources, as well as the support of family and friends, as she went through radiation, chemotherapy, and surgery. The cancer was now gone, and that was why she was completely taken by surprise when during a prophylactic round of chemotherapy, she had an emotional meltdown. The tears started and would not stop.

Maryanne and I are friends, so she was not surprised when her father, who had passed years before, weighed in on what was happening.

DAD: Maryanne, we are all with you. We love you and we are here helping in any way we can.

MARYANNE: I know. I can feel that. I'm so grateful.

DAD: Your family members who had this kind of cancer in the past did not survive. You are breaking the pattern. You're healing yourself, but, in doing so, you're offering healing to all of us.

MARYANNE: I can feel that. I'm turning around the old pattern by surviving. So why am I crying? I'm so grateful and happy at the same time.

DAD: We all have our ways of dealing with emotion and grief. You know how Mom dealt with it. She would drink to push her pain away. She self-medicated.

MARYANNE: I know.

DAD: So you took the high road. You consciously modeled after me. You're like me, an academic, a teacher, one who brings light to the world.

MARYANNE: I hope so.

DAD: I'll tell you something that will help you be even more compassionate to your mother. We both do the same thing she did! I also numbed my grief and sorrow. I intellectualized them away! That type of self-medicating is not frowned upon. In fact, it's condoned and considered smart and charming.

But think about it. I used my logic to disengage from my issues. I hid behind my intellect. My mind would tell me that sorrow and grief were not logical. They can't help anyway, so why give in to them? A lot of smart people are pretty proud of themselves for getting through things without giving in to tears. But that really is not as smart as I used to think.

You're determined to change our family history with this disease to one of survival. But curing a disease needs to take into account the lack of ease. You're curing the disease, but what about the attending fear, grief, and sorrow? You need to address those, too, to honor the mind, body, and soul connection.

You see, I avoided that connection, just like your mother did. Your mother did it through alcohol. Me, through logic.

MARYANNE: Wow!

DAD: You didn't realize that. I have news for you. Neither did I! I had no idea! So that's why I need you to know that expressing your emotions, letting yourself cry, is so important. You can't just talk about how you feel and explain it away. You have to actually emote. The brain alone can't do it. You need to literally allow the emotion to leave your body, just like the cancer. When the cancer goes, all that grief needs to go with it. You need to cry, the kind of crying that little kids do, with your nose running and stomach heaving.

MARYANNE: I've been like that all day!

DAD: That's good. Stay with it and let it go until it's gone. I think understanding all of this helps us to be more compassionate with Mom's issues. After I passed, I realized that I similarly dodged my pain and emotion. I just did it in a socially acceptable way.

I don't want you stuffing your pain inside you like both of your parents did. Purge and let it out. As this dis-ease is let go from your body, allow the emotion to go with it.

This is how you heal not only yourself, but also those who came before you. Your healing makes us happy, of course. But there is more. The way you are bringing consciousness to the dis-ease and releasing the attending emotion will affect all of us. Your entire soul family rises in consciousness along with you.

It's interesting, your emotion today, which you thought was out of the blue, helps me realize how much emotion I repressed in myself. You see, we are with you, watching you, feeling you, and healing along with you.

MARYANNE: That's amazing. Thank you!

DAD: Oh, and that beautiful dog. [Maryanne's dog had passed just a couple of months earlier.]

MARYANNE (WITH A NEW WAVE OF TEARS): I think about her, I feel her, every day!

DAD: But you didn't cry about her till now!

MARYANNE: You're right. I get it, thank you! And I can feel all of you helping me. Okay, I can do it. It's okay to cry.

Maryanne's dad wants us to realize that his choices of armor—intelligence and wit—protected him from being vulnerable.

DAD: My tactics were so covert and of course I didn't realize what I was doing. I actually thought that I had to "dumb it down" for people sometimes. The truth is, after I passed, I had to learn to "dumb it down" for myself to remember my humanness!

He stops to laugh at the irony. "My arrogance was purely a device to cover my vulnerability, which, of course, has its roots in fear."

MARYANNE IS learning, with her father's help, that vulnerability is not to be shunned. In fact, if we are open and honest about our fears and offer our truth to others, they in turn will usually have an empathic response. This reaction can bring us closer as we share the parts of ourselves that we work so hard to keep hidden. Because in reassuring others, we are reassuring ourselves. The reciprocity we have for each other can bring us a kinder, more compassionate reexamination of ourselves as we mirror each other's humanness.

So often souls channel in that they didn't understand, or even know, the extent of their fear of emotion and vulnerability. They go through exactly what we are going through when we question why we didn't say "I love you" more often before a loved one passed or have had more conscious and intimate conversations. So many of us, in body and out, are simultaneously going over the past and wondering why we were not more upfront with our truth.

Since we're going through this along with our out-of-body loved ones, why not help them, as they want to help us?

Right now, they are with us and can hear us. Right now, you can ease your burden as you help lift theirs. Tell them what you couldn't, offer the part of yourself that you might otherwise hold tight. Whether or not this immediately leads to forgiveness, for yourself or for them, the conversation is open. You are acknowledging your own desire for healing. Sharing this with them acknowledges that we are aware of the mirror effect we have with each other. Of course, your conversation acknowledges their viability and continued consciousness as well. This comforting truth can give all of us the courage needed to cut through how they, or we, disappointed each other, and ourselves, and lead us to releasing guilt and shame. This clearing leads us to explore and understand the underlying intention.

However hard the circumstances, if we set the intention that love is greater than our pain, we are led to the higher vibration that is the support and foundation of our healing.

CHAPTER 11

Healing After Suicide

The pain of having someone we love transition out of body is tough enough. Trying to understand why someone would end their life on this plane of his or her own volition opens a whole other can of worms. Those of us left behind are burdened with a lot of questions, along with all the grief that accompanies the physical loss, and often a sense of futility about the possibility of having those questions answered.

Helplessness and despair may manifest as anger.

- What the hell was he thinking?
- She knows I wanted to help her.
- Why didn't he tell us he was so unhappy?
- Why didn't she listen to my advice?
- I told him to get help.

Asking these kinds of questions and applying our own logic in an effort to understand the motivation behind an apparent suicide may feel like the only way our practical minds can grasp or cope with such a devastating act. In addition, it is not unusual for people to feel let down because someone they love made such an enormous decision without considering how it would affect those left behind.

- How could he do this to me?
- She knew she could talk to me.
- That was just plain selfish.
- He doesn't care if we're devastated.
- She didn't want to face her problems.
- Sure, that was a quick cure for him, but what about us?
- What am I supposed to do now?

This train of thought can trigger even more anger. It helps to remember that it is natural to try to process the loss from our own perspective. The emotional patterns following a loved one's suicide may be similar to the coping mechanisms we employ when dealing with any loss: we feel anger that it happened and anger at our helplessness. That anger may be the driving force, for some time, and it may well help us to anchor ourselves and release our grief.

But as we move beyond the shock and anger, many of us find compassion for the loved one who has passed. Rather than blaming them, we may move on to blaming ourselves. The guilt of not having been aware of a loved one's pain or able to help alleviate it amplifies the grief.

- If I only knew.
- I was oblivious.
- How could I be so blind?
- I let her down.
- If I only did [fill in the blank], they would still be here.

- I wasn't enough to make him happy.
- I didn't handle things well.

It is not unusual to feel any or all of the above and a whole lot more. The question is, can we find our way to being compassionate toward ourselves and apply the truth that love is greater than pain?

The grief of such a sudden and devastating loss is overwhelming. The heart is broken as the mind goes into a tailspin. We can stay in this reactive state of energy if we make that choice, consciously or unconsciously. For a time we might feel as if we don't have a choice.

After I channeled for the parents of a son who had committed suicide and who begged his parents not to feel guilt, the father plainly stated, "I will feel guilty every day for the rest of my life." I can tell you that his son is not happy with his father's decision. The young man's father may be unable to comprehend at this point that his emotional state actually affects his son. Clearly, his suffering is a result of his love for his son, and his desperate desire to have him back in his physical body. If he could extend that love to be able to hear what his son asks of him now, he would realize that his well-being remains important to his son. *The relationship is reciprocal!* When the father allows his love to be greater than his pain, he helps his son while helping himself.

∞

LEARNING THE underlying intention behind a suicide and understanding what was happening for our loved one at the time of transition is helpful to our healing, and theirs, and is available to us through channeling.

I've channeled many souls who brought about their own transition. Usually, I'll feel a flood of energy in my hands as they come through, signaling the fact that the spirit was released from the body through their own hands. But sometimes I won't feel that, as the soul may not have been planning to leave the body at all and does not feel responsible for his or her death.

Circumstances vary, but in every case I believe that understanding the big picture from our loved one's perspective opens the door to allow the love to flow between us and help ease the pain for all.

THROUGH CHANNELING, I have learned that suicides fall into three categories:

- Inadvertent or accidental suicide
- Not fully conscious suicide, or the person was not in their right mind when it happened
- Purposeful suicide

Inadvertent Suicide

Chad

Chad was brilliant and fiercely independent. He prided himself on being self-sufficient, a challenge, as he had been blind since infancy. I didn't know this the first time he came through to his mother. Our first session was over the phone. Imagine my surprise at his mother's astonishment when Chad spent the first few minutes describing his mother's face in detail! It was important to him that she realize that the blindness was a part of his physical life reality, not his soul's reality. Of course, his mother was overjoyed to hear this. He was happy to share that his physical limitation had offered him an extraordinary opportunity to learn and grow. He felt no bitterness in looking back over his life.

Chad's major concern was that some people thought he had purposefully taken his own life. He needed his mother to know the truth. He reported to her that he had taken his prescription medications and lay down on his couch for a nap. He did not wake up and found himself outside his body and going into light.

Those closest to Chad assumed that he'd mixed up or took too much of his medication, a likely accident, they thought, since he couldn't see. Chad reassured his mother that this was not the case. In fact, he was slightly offended at the idea that he would make such a mistake.

CHAD: Mom, I knew what I was doing. I didn't screw it up. My body had a reaction from the drug interactions. I didn't do anything on purpose, or even by accident, but people think so because I was blind. They think I mixed things up or maybe I thought life was so hard that I didn't want to be here anymore. That's just not true. I just took the pills I was supposed to take.

It was really weird because I took a nap and the next thing I knew I was looking all around. I was mesmerized. I could see everything in the room, and that was pretty cool, but then I saw me! I was lying on the couch, and then I realized what had happened. I didn't do it on purpose. I wouldn't do that to you or to me!

Mom: I knew it! It had to be that. He would never hurt himself and he's too much of a perfectionist to make that kind of mistake.

Chad: I felt bad about it, but it isn't like I feel guilty or anything. No one else should feel guilty either. It wasn't anyone's fault.

Chad went on to talk about what he learned and accomplished in his life and how much he appreciated his mother's support in his quest for independence.

I've learned through channeling that Chad's story is not unusual. A large percentage of transitions that are considered suicide are nothing of the sort. Pharmaceuticals save lives, but how they affect each individual body can vary, especially when combined with other medications.

Randy

Randy had no intention of taking his life. In fact, he was an avid surfer who was looking forward to a long-awaited vacation. His family was shocked when they came home one day and found that he had purposefully harmed himself. A belt was around his neck.

Randy (to his parents): It was so stupid. I don't know what the hell happened! I didn't do it on purpose! I don't even really remember what was going on.

Dad: Did you take anything? Were you on drugs?

Randy: Oh, Dad, you know I'm not on drugs . . . just the regular stuff. (Randy was taking two prescription drugs long-term to regulate chronic health issues.)

DAD: I just don't understand. What else was going on? Did you feel sick or anything like that?

RANDY: Wait a minute! I was getting a cold and someone at school gave me some cold stuff to take.

DAD: What was it?

RANDY: I don't know, just stuff for a cold. Oh, I guess that was pretty stupid considering I take other stuff. I'm sorry! I'm really sorry! I didn't do anything on purpose.

RANDY'S DAD did some research and found that the particular combination of drugs that Randy ingested might have caused several side effects, including hallucinations. Randy was not in his right mind and completely unconscious of what he was doing at the time of his transition. His actions were not the result of his intention. While Randy's parents grieve for their son, it helps them to know what happened. Randy's last thoughts, while in body, were not of sadness and desperation.

WHILE IT is normal for the logical mind to pick up the available pieces and try to make some kind of sense of what happened, looking at the outward circumstances of a loved one's transition can lead us to conclusions that are just not true.

Charlie

Charlie had just had a fight with his girlfriend. He stormed out of her apartment and got into his car to drive home. His car was later found wrapped around a tree. There were no other vehicles involved. I channeled Charlie for his mom.

MOM: Why? Why did you do that? I know you were mad, but it probably would have blown over. I don't understand it! They did an autopsy and you had beer in your system, but not nearly enough to be drunk. So you knew what you were doing!

CHARLIE: Mom, Mom, I didn't do anything! My girlfriend thinks I did it on purpose, too. I didn't! A squirrel ran out in front of me and I swerved so I wouldn't hit it. That's what really happened! I wasn't so mad that I would do that on purpose. We kind of fight a lot. She should know better and now you do! You have to tell her. I love her, and you! I wasn't looking to leave.

THIS SCENARIO would never have entered Charlie's mother's mind. Even though she now gets upset whenever she sees a squirrel, she says she takes comfort in the fact that Charlie's transition was the result of his soft-heartedness, and not his anger.

I WAS shocked when I learned through years of channeling how many apparent and deliberate-looking suicides are not intentional. Patterns started to emerge that can bring great comfort to those left behind. It is important for our peace of mind, and theirs, that we know what happens to the soul after it is released from the body, especially in this circumstance.

I have never witnessed or heard any indication that Divine Consciousness is cruel to the soul that leaves the body of its own volition. At the same time, I have never channeled a soul that is glad to have done it. How the soul processes and experiences transition and life review depends on the soul's own intention. For Chad, Randy, Charlie, and countless others, the soul that leaves the body unintentionally is treated with loving care and compassion. The newly transitioned soul is still greeted by loved ones who have passed before them. This is especially helpful, as it is normal, under the circumstances, for the soul to be initially shocked and upset by what has happened.

As I write this, a gathering of souls who have had this experience are looking over my shoulder. They want to tell you that their reaction to the event was similar to that of their loved ones on the physical plane. When they realized, out of body, what had happened, they were shocked and dismayed. Again, though circumstances may look otherwise, their transition was a total surprise. Usually their first thought, once they realize what has happened, is for us. Imagine their frustration as they see and hear our reactions. Their love for us overshadows their own pain. It is not unusual for them to find that their empathic response to our dismay becomes their driving emotion, causing more frustration than the transition itself.

The accidental suicide has a lot to contend with. Though the soul is surrounded by love and support, a wide range of emotions is released. Here are some honest first reactions as reported to loved ones through channeling:

- I can't believe I did that!
- That was so stupid of me.
- My mom's going to kill me!

- Oh #*@$! What the f#*@!
- Oh my God! I have to tell them what happened!

Thankfully, there is immediate help available. As we know, after the soul passes into the light, family members who have already passed, guides, and higher-vibrational loving beings step right up to help. In this circumstance, they also assure the new arrival that they understand that the transition to the spiritual plane was not deliberate. The disoriented soul is then shown that there is access to the loved ones left behind. They are encouraged when they learn that they will have help in finding ways to comfort them and lead them to learn the truth, that they had no plan to leave the body when they did.

Clearly, when their focus is on us, their love is greater than their own pain. When we realize that beyond the shock, anger, and dismay, our distress is the result of our loving the person who has passed, we align ourselves to help them.

Love is the driving force. We love them and they love us. When we offer them our help, we are allowing our love to be greater than our pain. You can do this right now. Talk to them! Offer up your own theories, and your fears. Admit to your frustration and helplessness. Your loved one may be feeling the same way. Remember, there is no death for the soul. Eventually, you will be with your loved ones in the same vibrational field, and able to fully and consciously embrace and share all.

What can you do in the meantime?

Continue to tell your loved one how you feel. They receive every word! You can comfort yourself as you comfort them. They need to know, whether you know what they were thinking when it happened or not, that you still love them. Of course you do. That's why you are in so much pain. This admission may provide the impetus for the transitioned soul to calm down and receive the help that is offered to them on the spiritual plane. We can help ease their guilt and open the door to conscious communication. Acknowledging that we are aware that they are trying to find ways to help us as they heal themselves accelerates the process. The love and help are reciprocal.

Unconscious Suicide

Having a clear idea of our loved one's intention has a powerful impact on our own healing. We have to remember that the brain is subject to fluctuations and impairment. So many people have channeled in, after bringing about their own transition, that they were not in their "right mind" when it happened. Some are not even conscious that they have done it. If our chest hurts, our logical mind will direct us to go to the doctor or hospital; but when the brain is injured or impaired, we lack the logical instruction it can provide. Instead of reaching out to others and seeking help, the person may have an overwhelming desire to just make the pain stop. Whether that pain is emotional or physical, impaired thinking can convince the person that they just need to put an end to it by any means available. The brain's function that understands that "this too shall pass" is replaced with the conviction that the pain will never end. The soul who transitions in this state is usually as stunned as we are.

Jon

When I channeled Jon for his mom, he was upbeat and energetic. The personality coming through did not match up with the profile of someone who had committed suicide. But he had, and in a manner that seemed quite deliberate, which he described in detail to his mother.

JON: Mom, everything is fine. No one is mad at me here. It's like if someone has a heart attack, you don't get mad at them for that. Well, Mom, I had a head attack, the same way a person can have a heart attack. Something in my head was broken and my brain wasn't functioning right. Don't blame yourself or me! The brain is part of the body, just like any other part, except when your brain is a little broken, then you can't use it to fix things and it gets all messed up. I'm okay now, and I love you, and I'm learning to forgive myself. And I need you to forgive yourself because it wasn't your fault.

JON CLEARLY has done his homework and understands his truth. We can only imagine his relief in getting this through to his mom. As painful as his transition was, for himself and for his loved ones, recognizing his intention has released him from excessive suffering and guilt. His desire is to share that understanding and help his loved ones release their own suffering and grief as well.

Evan

The moment Barbara sat down for her session, I could see a smiling young man at her side. Evan couldn't wait to tell his mom that he was fine and with her father. He shared that guidance and support were available for him, but he felt it was needed more for the people he'd left behind on the physical plane. He desperately wanted to explain the circumstances of his transition from his perspective, with the hope of alleviating at least some of his loved ones' pain.

Evan told his mother that his brain had an impairment that was not to be confused with his father's ongoing depression. He felt that he did not inherit this condition from his dad. In fact, he insisted that depression was not a factor at all. Yet he did realize that when he was in the physical body, his head sometimes did not function properly. He confided that he had frequent headaches while in his body, and when that happened, his thinking would become muddled. He admitted that his impaired thinking had led him to believe that standard types of medication would not help him. This shed understanding on his tendency to self-medicate with alcohol and cannabis. He explained that he was a popular guy who loved to be with his friends. When self-medicated, he felt normal and could enjoy the social gathering.

In Evan's description of his transition, his mother was in close proximity but not in the room when it happened.

EVAN: I felt a pop inside my head. I think it was always there, like a physical thing, and it was just going to happen at some point. In a way, I was surprised I'd lasted so long and it hadn't happened sooner. There was this pop, no pain, and then I saw Grandpa, your dad, right in front of me! Well, I kind of realized what that meant right away. I love him, and since he died, I really missed him.

Mom, you came running and started yelling and I turned to see what was going on. Grandpa put his hand on my face and turned it toward him so I didn't see what you were upset about. He told me to go with him and I did. All these people were hugging me and everything was okay.

Mom, you have to know what really happened. My brain just kind of popped and I was outside myself and everything is okay. You don't have to worry about me.

Evan's mom hung on every word and said it made perfect sense.

Evan: Mom, if my heart blew up or an organ ruptured, no one would question my motivation. My head popped, that's the only way I can put it.

Evan's mother then told about the transition from her point of view. She heard the "pop," ran into the room, and found that her son had indeed had his head "pop" from a self-inflicted bullet wound. Evan had taken his own life.

Evan: But that's not what happened from inside me. And that's why Grandpa literally turned my face away. I never saw what you saw! I wasn't conscious of what I did! I just was making the pain stop.

Everyone out here is helping me. I know it would have been better to get help and stuff in a different way. But the brain can be tricky. If you hurt a part of yourself, you can use your brain to get help or figure out how to fix it. If your brain is messed up, like really badly, you sometimes don't know what you're doing.

That's why you were so shocked. I was fine a lot of the time. I had all these plans. I wasn't looking to leave.

I don't hate you or Dad or anything like that. I don't hate myself, either. My only thought was to make the pain stop. I know I couldn't think straight sometimes. I think you know that, too. But, Mom, I didn't know how to fix it while I was still in my body. Like I said, I realize now that my brain was impaired, like partly broken. And, Mom, it was physical! It wasn't 'cause I was sad or mad or anything like that.

So, you have to know, Grandpa and everyone out here really helped me. I went 'cause I had something physically broken, not emotionally broken. I hear people talk to you about it and I need you to know the truth from my point of view, what really happened. And, Mom, I know that you know! I don't think you're surprised by this at all!

Though she was crying, Evan's mom was also smiling.

MOM: I knew it! It totally makes sense. I knew he wasn't in his right mind and wouldn't have done that if he was.

EVAN: Exactly!! I don't remember doing it! It's just not what I thought I was doing.

EVAN REPORTS now that everything is different for him since his parents know the truth.

EVAN: I felt so bad that they felt so bad. I just wanted to get through to them. But, you know, I kind of knew that my mom was starting to get it. She would be crying sometimes, and sometimes she would just look up and say, "Why Evan, why?" And then I would hug her, and I know she could feel that I love her even if she wasn't aware of what I was doing. I just kept hugging her over and over, and even if she didn't really know what was going on, I think she was starting to feel better.

I can tell you, I know she misses me and everything, but she's so much better because she knows, and, of course, that makes me feel better!

⟨⟩

If you're reeling or recovering from a loved one's suicide, look up, ask, and listen.

If your loved one passed from an unconscious or unintended suicide, they are conscious now and very likely looking to reassure you. Remember, if you try to allow the beauty and love around you to permeate your devastation, you will raise your vibration and increase the availability of your loved one to get through to you. This, of course, is not so easy at times, especially when honoring and allowing the grief process. Try to connect with nature, look out the window, pet an animal, listen to and admire birds, and allow others to hug and help you. While these things might feel minor or ineffectual in light of the depth of your pain, they will change and lighten your energy field, and the effects are cumulative.

Look at it this way. Would you want your loved one who has passed to not open up to the love and healing available to them? They want the same for us. The result is more communication, peace, and healing for all.

. . .

HOWEVER HARD the circumstances, if we decide that love is greater than our pain, the healing happens, both for them and for us.

Purposeful Suicide

In my many years of channeling, I have come across very few people who purposefully took their physical lives. And I have yet to meet someone who is happy they did so.

Usually, a purposeful suicide goes directly into a rehab setting to help the soul understand why it would choose to go against its own life force. Intention is taken into consideration. Everything I have witnessed through channeling demonstrates that loving-kindness is directed to the soul. If something darker exists out there, I haven't experienced it. Of course, I am protected from any energy or entity that is not high vibration and communicating for the highest good and for healing purposes. This is because I state my intention when I begin channeling and ask for protection.

I can't stress enough how important doing this is. I don't do it because I'm afraid of anything negative. Rather, reiterating and asking for the highest vibrational communication aligns me with the big picture of Divine Consciousness positivity. Though I'm often accused of being a Pollyanna type of person, I can't deny the negativity perpetuated by some people on the Earth's physical plane. Just as I might not choose to go wandering about alone after dark without accompaniment, the same goes for the spiritual plane. I ask Divine Consciousness and the high-vibrational beings that support it to protect, guide, and align me, and all I come in contact with, to the highest good.

I recommend that you do the same in whatever fashion you are comfortable with. I reiterate this here, as it would be helpful to increase this type of support when trying to understand and wade through the possibly negative thoughts and motivation of one who has left intentionally.

Purposeful suicides seem to fall into several categories based on intention.

- You're better off without me.
- I'm better off leaving.
- I want to be with someone else who has transitioned.
- Frustration and inability to move forward.
- Guilt over a true or perceived wrong.
- Retaliation, wanting to hurt others.

But of course, there are many motivations. Every soul has its own story.

Gary

You're Better Off Without Me

Gary always put his family first. He worked hard to take care of them, but admitted when he channeled in to his wife that during his physical life he had trouble with emotional intimacy. He was taught, and believed, that his love and devotion were demonstrated by his work ethic and ability to provide his family with all of their physical needs. His wife and two sons understood this and did not feel deprived, as Gary was a warm, humorous, and supportive presence, even as he was uncomfortable with displays of affection.

So it came as a shock when Gary's body was found in his office, and the autopsy revealed a lethal level of prescription drugs.

SALLY (GARY'S WIFE): Why, Gary, why would you do that? I thought you were happy. I thought we were happy. At first, I thought that maybe you had a double life or an addiction, but I know that's just not true. Why didn't you come to me?

GARY: I'm sorry, I should have come to you, but I couldn't put you through it.

SALLY: What are you talking about? Put me through what?

GARY: I went to the doctor a couple of times. I just went while I was at work. I didn't want anyone to worry until I knew what I was dealing with. Once I knew, I just couldn't tell you, or say it at all. Every day I would look at you and the kids, and know that what I knew would ruin everything. I couldn't stand to destroy our family and have everyone be sad watching me die. I just couldn't allow that. I take care of you, not the other way around.

SALLY: What!? You can tell me anything. I love you.

GARY: I know. I love you, too. And I'm sorry. I was just never comfortable talking about that stuff. But you know.

SALLY: I do. But I still don't know what you're talking about.

GARY: Sally, I was sick, and it was just going to get worse. I was supposed to go back to the doctor. I called and told her that I switched to another doctor, so she wouldn't try to check up on me.

I just couldn't do it, and I thought everyone would be better off if I kept it quick and simple. Obviously, I didn't think it through. I did it because I love you. Believe me, it's true!

SALLY (CRYING): We could have gone through it together! You have people who love you! You didn't have to die alone.

GARY (CRYING): I know. I get it now. But all I could think of was you and the kids watching me lie there. I didn't want you to see that.

You know I'm not so gracious when it comes to letting people do things for me. I pictured what it would be like and I just couldn't let that happen.

I'm sorry, I'm so sorry.

SALLY: Are you okay? I love you! Are you okay?

GARY: Yeah, I realized pretty early on that maybe it wasn't the smartest thing to do. I swear I was only trying to save you from pain, but I saw what happened, how you reacted when you found out. I hadn't thought of that. I didn't realize or think that part through.

SALLY (WHISPERING): No, you didn't.

GARY: I'm so sorry.

SALLY: But are you okay? Are you okay now?"

GARY: Well, my dad was right there to meet me. He didn't seem mad or anything. He just held his arms out and I went with him. I could see you and the kids. You didn't know yet, and then I went into light.

Frankly, I was surprised I was still alive. I thought that when you die, you were done. I thought I was just going to sleep and that's it. So it took me a minute to get acclimated.

Then all these therapist types are around me, and they stay with me, while I see what looks like a movie about my life. It was a little confusing, because while it looked like I was doing all the right things, I think that I might have been on autopilot. I was pretty busy, but not really talking about or sharing what I felt. I think I was just happy when I was doing it, because I believed that was all I was supposed to do. I realize now that I missed a lot of what was going on, because I wasn't that engaged.

The people, or guides, or whatever you call them out here, helped me understand that while I'm okay out here, by doing what I did, I missed an opportunity to learn how to receive.

At first, I wasn't on board with that, because I just didn't want you and the kids to suffer.

Now I realize, and I was stubborn about it at first, that my diagnosis was an opportunity to open up. They showed me how vulnerability can open things up. I hadn't thought of it that way. We all could have learned things and gotten closer.

I'm sorry. I meant well, I really did. I just didn't know how the whole emotional thing worked.

SALLY (LAUGHING): You never knew how the whole emotional thing worked! And I loved you anyway! This is just so like you. I never realized, never even thought of the possibility. All I could think was that you weren't happy.

GARY: I know.

SALLY: I love you!

GARY: I love you, too.

SALLY: God, I wish you could have said that every now and then when you were here.

Gary: I know. I know that now.

Eddie

I'm Better Off Leaving

Eddie has been out of body for a while. More than twenty-five years after what appeared to be an intentional suicide by a drug overdose, his sister, Janet, had a session, wanting to talk to her newly transitioned mother to possibly find out why her exuberant and apparently life-loving brother had taken his own life.

MOM: Thank you! Thank you for taking such good care of me! [Janet had been the primary caretaker as her mother's health deteriorated from lung cancer.] You were right there. Thank you for everything. You're an angel!

JANET: You're okay now? Everything's okay?

MOM: Oh yes! I'm with my mother and father. And your brother is right here, I saw him even before I went! I was still in bed. I had that oxygen on and I was just lying there and then I see him just floating above me. Janet, he looked so good!

JANET: That makes sense. He always did!

MOM: When I first saw him, I was confused and thought I might be going crazy. But right behind him were my parents! They were all smiling at me and I felt wonderful! I knew then that everything would be okay. They were so happy to see me, and I knew it was right to go with them.

JANET: I'm so glad Eddie's all right. You must be so happy!

MOM: Oh yes! And now I know what happened.

JANET: Really?

MOM: Eddie didn't want to go. He just thought it was best considering the circumstances.

JANET: What circumstances?

EDDIE: Hi, honey! I'm here. Thank you for praying for me all these years.

JANET: Oh, Eddie! You're there? I always worried about you after you did what you did. You're not supposed to do that!

EDDIE: I know, I know. But there's something you don't know. Mom knows it now and wants me to tell you. I had AIDS.

JANET (CRYING): You know, that crossed my mind. I mean, I thought you were pretty happy, so I figured there might be something else going on.

EDDIE: Well, yeah! Look at all my friends who were dying back then. [A crowd of young men gathered behind Eddie.] I saw what happens. I saw what they looked like, and I was like, "Hell, no!" Oh, you can say "hell" out here! It's kind of a joke, 'cause so many people said that that's where we're going. Well, God loves us, even if some people don't.

JANET: So you're okay?

EDDIE (LAUGHING): Hell yeah! I just decided I wasn't going to go through that. Back then it was a death sentence anyway. Why wait and suffer? But, you know, I think knowing what I know now, that I could have done it differently.

JANET: You mean like telling us and letting us in, and letting us help you? Like letting us love you?

EDDIE: Yeah, I know, you're right. But I was scared. Do you remember what my friends looked like? I didn't want to look like that. I didn't want to see that, let alone have you see that. So, I'm sorry. That's the whole story.

JANET: Well, I'm really glad you're okay now.

EDDIE: I'm really sorry I wasn't there to help with Mom. I watched you doing everything. I know you looked up a few times and got mad that I wasn't there to help.

JANET: I'm ashamed to say it, but you're right. I think it was more about being in it together, not about doing the actual stuff. I was happy to be able to help Mom.

EDDIE: I know. I get it. But I was always right there. Don't worry, I'll take over from here. [Eddie put his arm around his mom.]

JANET: Thank God! Okay, now I don't have to worry about either one of you!

EDDIE (LAUGHING): Let us worry about you! You need to get out more! And you need more rest . . . and fun!

JANET (LAUGHING): Oh God, I forgot how bossy you always were.

EDDIE: Oh, it's still me, Honey, it's still me!

EDDIE is not an anomaly in thanking loved ones for their prayers. He reports that he liked knowing that his sister was directing energy toward his well-being. That means, he says, that she knew he was somewhere, that he still existed and still mattered. As angry and devastated as she was, she was still his sister, still watching out for him, and still petitioning God on his behalf.

Julie

I Just Wanted to Be with Him

Julie was devastated after her boyfriend was killed in the cross fire of a gang-related drive-by shooting. Within days, she took her own life. Her mother knew how distraught her daughter was and was not totally taken by surprise. She hoped to hear that Julie was okay and reunited with her boyfriend.

JULIE: I'm sorry, Mom, I'm so sorry. I just didn't want to live without Joey. I couldn't do it.

MOM: I know, sweetheart, I understand.

JULIE: All I thought was that if I just did it, I could follow him. It wasn't his fault that any of it happened. He didn't even know most of those guys. I was scared for him and just wanted to help him. I didn't want to live without him.

MOM: I know.

JULIE: Please don't be mad. And, I know, you're just so sad. I'm sorry. I see you and I'm with you, and I'm so sorry.

MOM: I know, it's okay now. You're all right? Are you with God? Are you with Joey?

JULIE: Oh, Mom, it wasn't that easy. Everyone's nice and everything, but at first, I couldn't just go where I wanted. They showed me Joey and that he's okay, but first I had to look at why I stopped my own life. See, Joey didn't do that, but I did. Joey didn't plan on or want to go. But I did. So everyone here is nice and everything, and you feel all this love. But I had to go to these classes. I had to just look at me, not just Joey, to figure out why I would react that way. I know it was because I loved Joey, but they wanted me to realize that my own life still had a reason, some kind of purpose. I was there that night and didn't get killed, and I had to see that maybe I had more stuff to do, that I wasn't done yet. Joey didn't have a choice that day, but I had a choice, so I had to look at that.

So I did it to be with Joey, but it didn't work that way. I had to deal with me first. I think it must be like being in rehab. And now, I can see Joey. And you know what? First thing, he says he's sad I did it! He was so sad!

Mom: I knew he was a good boy!

Julie: I know. I get it now. I'm sorry, Mom.

Julie's mom was obviously devastated by her daughter's decision to follow Joey. Yet she offers Julie her compassion. Julie reports that she knows now that taking her own physical life was not the most appropriate decision. Her mother's empathy has helped her move beyond her disappointment in herself and has helped accelerate her healing.

Tim

I Couldn't Live with the Guilt

Tim was always careful with his guns. An avid hunter, he kept his weapons clean, oiled, and under lock and key. It never crossed his mind that his two sons, ages twelve and fifteen, along with their two friends, would find a way to get into that cabinet. They had been planning to do so for a few months, secretly watching their

dad when he locked up his guns and put away the key. Curiosity turned deadly when they finally had a chance to get into the
gun locker when their father wasn't home. A gun was accidentally
fired, causing a bullet to go through their younger friend, killing
him instantly. Of course, the surviving kids were beside themselves.
Both families were devastated. The victim's family filed a lawsuit.
Shortly after, the father who owned the guns hanged himself in the
room where the tragedy had taken place. Tim's wife, Mary, hoped
to hear from Tim and learn that he was all right and where she
hoped he should be. Her religious training left her concerned that
because of his suicide Tim would never have peace and be with
those who had passed before him.

MARY: I get it, I do! I know you couldn't live with the guilt. I understand. It felt like all our lives were over when that gun went off.
I just need to know, Timmy, are you with God?

   TIM: Yes, yes! I'm sorry. I just couldn't live with it.

   MARY: I know, but how do I deal with the kids? How do I teach
them to go on? I have to make sure they don't do what you did.
I mean, that's not the answer. I understand, but that just screwed
things up more. And now I'm worried about you and what happens
to you.

   Tim reaches behind him and brings someone forward. His
hands are resting on the shoulders of the boy who passed from the
gunshot, as he presents him to his wife.

   TIM: Yeah, we're both here! We're both okay.

   MARY (CRYING): Oh my God! Oh my God!

   TIM: Mary, he's right here. And I'm so sorry. I couldn't live with
the guilt. I realize I really just made it worse. I'm sorry I did it.

That's no example for the boys. They're having such a hard time and I'm not there to help you. Please forgive me. Tell them I want them to forgive me. It was selfish. I see that now. [He is now crying.] I promise to do everything I can to help everyone. I just wish I could take it back. I love you. Tell everyone we're okay. [He gestures to the boy, who is smiling.] He came to me and hugged me. He's not mad. He knows it was an accident. He wants you to tell his family. What a mess, huh? So horrible for everyone. And, I'm so sorry about everything. I always tried to be so careful. I love you so much. Tell everyone the truth, that we're both here, and together. We're healing, and we'll try to help everyone else do that, too.

Retaliation

Of the many readings I have done involving suicide, very few, in fact, only a couple, indicate that the life was taken with the intention of punishing or getting even with someone else. In these cases, relatives who are out of body, or loving guides, report that the person is in a rehab setting. They explain that the soul needs time to explore why its own life force, and desire to live, became secondary to the intention of hurting another. Rehab is kind, patient, and loving. The soul has the opportunity to examine what may lie behind the intended cruelty. Healing the pain that the person experienced while in body, which elicited the desire to hurt another human being, needs to be addressed before the soul is restored to autonomy.

At this time, a soul is not available for communication. The focus is on healing. When the soul has examined and understood that it was wrong to allow pain to be greater than love—when the primary goal is healing, love, and peace, for itself, and for others—it is free to be with the loved ones, both in and out of body. Healing is now expansive, and the soul, with its newfound understanding, can help those in pain on the physical plane who may be contemplating a similar action.

Compassion leads the way as the soul is realigned to truth, that love is greater than pain.

Purposeful Suicide with the Intention to Harm Others

After 9/11, I channeled for people who desperately wanted to know about their loved ones' final moments in body, and how they were faring on the spiritual plane. What came through, along with the smoke, noise, and fear, was story after story of people trying to help others. Many of them continued to do so even after they left their physical bodies. All of those I channeled wanted to reassure their loved ones that life continues on the spiritual plane and that they are conscious of our grief and shock.

One mother, after hearing from her son, who was on an upper floor of the second tower when it was struck, asked an interesting question, one that had never crossed my mind to ask. "What happens to the perpetrators?"

High-vibration guides immediately came through to answer and show us where they were. Those who chose to leave the physical body while murdering others did not pass into light. In fact, the only way to describe where they are is a total lack of light. I was shown this space, though I was not inside it. As I observed, I could feel that the energy of it was heavy, dark, and viscous. This was a stark contrast from the conscious high frequency coming through with the guide's explanation.

They are in here. They are unconscious.

While in body, they were separated from their minds.

What they did was not logical.

While in body, they were separated from their hearts.

The perpetrators lacked compassion and did not have empathy for the anguish and pain of their victims.

While in body, they were separated from their gut instinct.

The premeditated destruction of their physical bodies went against their own life force. They did not value their own breath.

Many do not even realize that their own consciousness survived physical death. They are allowed to stay here, in unconsciousness, as long as they would like. It is the soul's choosing.

The view started to change. I felt myself being pulled away. I was now above this dark abyss. From this vantage point, I could see many high-vibrational beings of light situated around the edges of the darkness. The guide continued:

> When they are ready and choose to go toward light, we
> are here, ready to help them face the extent of their soul's
> disengagement and destruction. In the meantime, they
> are guarded and unable to cause more harm to them-
> selves and others.

I like to use the analogy that my access to the spiritual plane feels like an open window, sometimes even an open door. I don't have, and wouldn't ask for, access to everything. I am comfortable with the information Divine Consciousness chooses to share through channeling. I always ask that all that I perceive and share be for healing purposes. Maybe that's why I find myself channeling out-of-body loved ones who know that shedding light on the circumstances of their suicide, or apparent suicide, will help heal the loved ones they left behind on the physical plane.

Clearly, there are people who purposefully cause harm to others. I'm not privy to everything that happens when they return to the spiritual plane. From what I have learned through channeling, I trust that the goal is the healing of the soul.

Processing grief is a complicated endeavor, compounded by so many circumstances. While emotional pain may be unavoidable, I am grateful that channeling provides clarity, helping to relieve unnecessary anguish.

CHAPTER 12

Our Animal Friends
and Reincarnation

Sharing our lives with animals is therapeutic on so many levels. Not only are they cuddly companions, they also vibrate at a high frequency. Science has long known the calming influence a dog or cat can have with people who suffer from anxiety or illness. They are in the present moment, and often demand our attention to share the moment with them. They are fine teachers when it comes time to relax. We have much to learn by observing their dedication to the basics. They are tuned in to their own needs. When they are tired, they sleep. When they are hungry, they let you know it. Best of all, unless they have had previous trauma, when they want to share their affection, they do so. They don't hide the way they feel. This can remind us to do the same. Their intention is not crowded with convoluted thought. What you see is what you get, and that's usually a whole lot of love.

When a furry family member passes, our world can be as shaken as when a human companion passes. There is so much to miss, from snuggle time to play time. Here's the good news. Our animal loved ones will often stay with us, similarly to our human loved ones.

THROUGH CHANNELING, we learn about the depth of their dedication, bond, and loyalty to us. We gain insight into their emotional world, and find that, just like us, they have clear ideas and preferences. They are attracted to and love to play in higher-vibrational frequencies. While my channeling experience is with domestic animals, I have no doubt that wild animals share in this energetic preference. If there is an in-body animal present when I channel, you can be sure that they will come as close as possible and bask in the high-frequency channeling energy. As a matter of fact, there is a cat draped on my legs as I write this!

Bob's Dog Tommy

Remember Bob from Chapter 4, who helped release his father's guilt? After his dad and sweetheart came through, we had another visitor. Bob's session took place in Los Angeles at the home of my casting director friend and her canine companion, Leo, a Petit Basset Griffon Vendéen. I often visit L.A. and will usually do some channeling sessions while I'm there. Leo loved it when I did. He reminded me of the shaggy and friendly dog, Barkley, on *Sesame Street*. Whenever I would channel, Leo made it his practice to come sit on my feet. Most clients didn't mind. In fact, they usually found it calming. Bob, a dog lover, was no exception.

The dog sat quietly on my feet through most of the session, gently snoring his way through it, as was his norm. But today, Leo was about to have a little social adventure; Bob and I witnessed the energetic exchange, as we had the opportunity to observe what probably takes place all the time.

When Bob's human loved ones were done communicating, we had a visit from Tommy, an out-of-body bulldog who presented himself and sat on the floor right next to Bob's feet. Leo, the in-body dog, immediately lifted his head and sniffed. As Tommy communicated to Bob, Leo got up and walked over to Tommy and circled him, sniffing every inch of him! The in-body dog fully acknowledged the out-of-body dog!

Channeling a dog is a pretty interesting experience. Because they are nonverbal, I'll see a series of pictures as shown through their eyes, and I'll feel their physicality superimposed on my own. This is not unusual when channeling a person, especially a child. Channeled words are only one aspect of the multilayered communication. Intention and detail come across through pictures, physical sensations, and waves of emotion and energy. So while channeling a dog is not that different from channeling a person, there might be a variation in the physical cues I pick up. I will actually perceive what it feels like to be inside the dog's body. It's not jarring, as we have most of the same physical parts, though I do admit that it is fun to learn what it feels like to have a wagging tail! I am aware of the presence of guides helping me translate the physical cues into words that I can relay to the person I'm channeling for. This is familiar to me as it is consistent with the interpretive support that comes through when I'm channeling someone who speaks another language. In that situation, I hear snippets of the other language, and immediately hear the translation. I will explain that this is happening, as this is an identifying factor. That said, I do not hear or channel barking, meowing, or other animal sounds. I assume that this is because the recipient of the channeling does not usually understand that mode of communication. Even if they did, they wouldn't make sense of it coming from me!

Tommy wanted to thank Bob for helping him leave his body when the time was right for him to go. He had been in pain but did not want to disappoint Bob by passing. Bob's love was greater than his pain when he put Tommy's needs first. Tommy knew this and was filled with gratitude. He projected the scenario and I could see it in my mind as if I were watching a movie. The veterinarian helped Tommy release from his body and Bob held him lovingly all the way through it.

This was just the beginning. Tommy had a lot to relay. He planned to come back as Bob's dog again, he communicated, but he wanted to be a little different the next time around. He shared his perception that while he was fully loved and enjoyed a wonderful life with Bob, he would have appreciated better reactions from people he would meet when he and Bob were out for their walks. Tommy loved children, but his sweetness could be overshadowed by his physical presence, which often frightened them. Just when Tommy was about to make a new human friend, he would receive a confusing response. Most people would pull back, and a few times children cried and ran away. Tommy didn't like this at all. Bob knew exactly what Tommy was talking about. He had witnessed this reaction himself when Tommy would turn his big bulldog head and reveal a severe and drooling underbite and big bulging eyes. Bob was not surprised by Tommy's admission. He had always suspected that Tommy was somehow aware of his circumstances. Bob reassured Tommy that he was always beautiful in his eyes, and that he would welcome him for another go-around in whatever doggy form Tommy chose.

During this communication, Leo, the in-body dog, continued to circle and sniff at the out-of-body dog. When Tommy was done channeling, and his energy dissipated as he left, Leo stretched out in the warm energetic spot that Tommy had just vacated.

TOMMY'S VISIT illuminates several comforting concepts. First and foremost, our animal friends will usually stay with us after they pass. Of course, we know that our love for them lives on in our hearts. But how comforting it is to know that our furry pals continue to love us as well! Animals report, through channeling, that they still curl up in their favorite spots. If your animal friend was not allowed on your bed while in body, there is a pretty good chance that that rule is now broken. We may not be able to see these out-of-body animals, but other animals can. Leo made it very clear that he was able to see and smell Tommy. Because the vibration was high and Tommy's intention was to share his love and gratitude, Leo did not pick up anything that threatened or disturbed him. Quite the opposite! Leo was so comfortable with Tommy's presence that he occupied the space that held Tommy's residual energy.

So if in-body animals can see out-of-body animals, do they also see out-of-body people? Yes! The out-of-body animals share the higher-frequency vibrational level where out-of-body loved ones reside.

Remember Patty and Bill in Chapter 6? Bill advised his wife to adopt the two dogs that he would arrange to bring to her. Bill wanted to utilize the dog's high-frequency ability to show his wife that he was present—one of the dogs would often seem to be barking at nothing by the front door, though as Bill explained to Patty through channeling, in reality the dog was acknowledging his presence.

So many children, channeling in to their parents, will describe the family pet and the strange behavior the family has been witnessing since the child's physical passing. Cats and dogs may look like they are chasing or trying to catch something we cannot see. They might stare or jump at a fixed spot right beside us. Out-of-body children channel in that the animals are seeing and responding to them as they get the animals' attention and play with them. Like Bill, the children are demonstrating several truths. The children's knowledge of their animal friends' particular behaviors affirms that their own memory is intact after passing, and their descriptions of the pet's behavioral changes, after the child's passing, proves that the child is home with their family in real time. How else would they know? The best part is that an animal's unusual behavior is a direct result of the pet's continued love and communication with the loved one who has passed. Our knowledge of this broadens our perception. Out-of-body loved ones, especially kids, still have fun playing with the family pet. In addition to the joy, the experience or intention is often to set up a signal system with which the animal can alert the in-body people that their out-of-body loved one is present.

Out-of-body loved ones sometimes come around and share some of the things they enjoyed while they were in body. Many out-of-body people, especially children, like to continue certain rituals. If the family, or siblings, watched a favorite TV show together, the one who is now out of body will often channel in that they are still present and enjoying it with them. Several times, I have channeled an out-of-body person's opinion about who won on TV talent shows! These conversations can be pretty interesting with the out-of-body person talking about their preferences in similar terms as they did when they were in body. If there is a pet present when our out-of-body loved one is enjoying a favorite show or activity with us, it is the perfect opportunity to pay attention to the animal's behavior. They may be a playful catalyst tipping everyone off to the fact that our out-of-body loved one is joining us.

RYAN, THE young man in Chapter 8 who brought us seventeen birds, channeled in that he knew his parents were puzzled by some of the family dog's unusual behavior that only manifested after Ryan's passing. Ryan described how the dog would go to the bottom of the stairs and look up and bark. His mother didn't put it together until Ryan pointed it out.

RYAN: Mom, remember how I would play with Taffy and she'd get so excited and keep barking? Well, I'm doing the same thing, and so is she! I call her over to the stairs so you can see that there's no other reason for her barking.

You can see that she's not barking because she wants you to do something, like let her out or give her a treat. She's just playing with and barking at me! And now you know what the deal is. She lets you know that I'm right there with you.

RYAN'S MOM: You know, I started to wonder about that! At first, I thought that maybe she was going a little crazy, or maybe it was grief that Ryan wasn't there. But it's because Ryan is there! Smart dog!

OBSERVE YOUR dog's, cat's, or other pet's behavior. They, like us, may be depressed as a result of missing the physical dynamic and rhythm of the life they shared with a loved one who has passed. At the same time, they probably are spending time staring at what appears to be nothing. Pay attention. Their high-frequency perception, which makes them capable of being catalysts for our own recognition of an out-of-body loved one's presence, is another reason, among many, to appreciate our animal companions.

MOST ANIMALS' life expectancies are much shorter than our own. During the time they are with us, they share so many of our emotions and often understand our intentions better than our human friends do. Most of our treasured animal companions, like Tommy, do not want to let us down by dying, even when they know that their transition time is near. An animal's instinct may be to crawl off and find a quiet place to be alone when the time comes to pass. This pull may become secondary when our animal's love and concern for us becomes greater than their own pain. If you have animals close to your own heart, you have already learned that they are empathic. Their concern for us can motivate them to override their own needs. One of the difficult challenges we face in our human lives is putting the suffering of those we love before our own feelings. Our love is greater than our pain when we tell our human and nonhuman loved ones that it's okay to go. We can share our understanding that, though they don't want to leave us, they really don't have a choice. Both humans and animals, channeling in, describe the relief they felt when their loved ones helped relieve them of guilt and stress as transition became imminent. Doing what we don't want to do, in an effort to relieve our animal friends of pain and suffering, is a kindness we do not need to feel guilty about. This is confirmed every time a beloved pet channels in their gratitude for our assistance in helping them let go.

When our family was faced with helping our sweet, loyal, and overly barky Australian cattle dog, Harlee, leave her body, the choice felt both obvious and difficult. She could no longer walk, eat, or drink, and was in constant pain. If we looked for guilt, it could be found only in not having helped her leave sooner. The veterinarian came to the house and after reassuring us that there was nothing else to be done and no potential for healing, he asked for Harlee's feline friends, our two cats, to come and say goodbye. We opened the door so they could come into the room. They slowly approached Harlee, sniffed her, and then settled down close by. I believe Harlee was aware of what was going on. Now, with her usual hyperactive behavior subdued, she purposefully looked into my husband's eyes, then mine, and gave us each one lick. She then rested her head on the floor, closed her eyes, and waited. She was calm and released a deep sigh. I could feel her presence with us for a few moments after she left her body. I understood that she was thanking us. Then I felt the exuberant Harlee energy returning. It was no longer suppressed by her pain-filled physical body. Now, a few years later, I still see her once in a while out of the corner of my eye.

Once they are out of body, our loved animal friends consistently channel in their appreciation, love, and gratitude. Either I will see them or a person who is channeling in will hold them up. Though we may dearly miss their physical form in so many ways, and they may miss our daily rituals, we don't need to worry about their missing us. Now in spirit form, animals stay with the in-body and out-of-body people and animals they love. Remember, our out-of-body animal companions have access to us, just as our out-of-body human loved ones do. They can see us and don't have to miss us or wonder if we still exist. Of course, like out-of-body people, they miss the physical life we shared with them. When I channel them, they will show their favorite people and activities. They may also visually project favorite memories, and doggies want me to add . . . treats! A lot of people channeling in will present pets they had in the past, and will share their delight that their out-of-body animal companions were part of their welcoming committee.

Animals may also project a visual image of a different animal that their human companion had years before. When I channel in the description and personality of the long-ago pet, the human who is listening will usually be quite surprised. They are then shocked to hear that the pet they are now grieving for was also that other long-gone companion! Through channeling, I have learned that many of us have strong bonds with particular animals who I believe are part of our soul family. Because our life expectancy is so much longer than that of our soul animals, they will come back to us, often several times, during our lifetime. They may stay out of body for as long as they like, but they have the option to come back through a shorter (for most animals) gestation period than our own, and go back to the familiar life they shared in their last incarnation. If we miss their animal companionship, and if we are eventually willing to introduce a new nonhuman companion into our lives, we may find that our new friend is really our old friend in a brand-new body. They may look different and sound different, but the soul and soul connection are the same.

Guides are laughingly pointing out that out-of-body animals will "sniff out" whether or not it is appropriate and good for all involved when considering a return to the people they love in a new physical body. How do they find us? They haven't strayed far. They resonate with us, and like our out-of-body loved ones, they will help pull us toward their, and our, best interests.

Missy

Celia, Jack's mom, made it a habit to bring her dogs to the park every morning. After Jack's passing, while they frolicked and sniffed, she would often be drawn to crystals and heart-shaped stones that were partially or almost completely buried in the dirt. She instinctively felt that Jack was presenting these gifts. On one particular morning, Celia received an unexpected surprise. When she and her canine companions reached their favorite spot, they came across a box of kittens! A woman, with a couple of kids in tow, had just discovered them. Both women expressed their disappointment in someone's cruelty in abandoning them and wondered what to do.

The kittens were all ridiculously cute and appealing. Having quite the menagerie at home, Celia was not looking to add to the collection. Then, one of them looked up into Celia's eyes. Of course the tiny calico kitty went home with Celia.

Several friends, myself included, came to Celia's home to witness newly named Missy's introduction to her new human and animal family. That tiny kitten sat in the middle of the room and took us all in. With a long glance at Celia, Missy made it clear that she was at home. Then she curled up and went to sleep.

As I marveled at Missy's comfort level, I channeled in a vision of a black-and-white cat. The information came in that this particular cat was close to Celia when she was a young child. This sweet soul companion had chosen to return to Celia and was now slumbering contentedly in front of us.

Celia was astounded to hear this. She had grown up on a working ranch and as a child felt most comfortable in the company of animals. Celia shared that she had a deep bond with a childhood black-and-white cat. She would often crawl into the remote hay-filled area of the barn where this cat chose to bear her kittens. Celia was always welcome and would spend much of her time cuddled up with them.

Missy acclimated quickly, and though Celia has loved many dogs and cats over the years, she is delighted with their deep bond. Now, several years later, Celia confides that she loves to bury her nose in Missy's fur. There, and only there, does she smell the old familiar scent of hay, and those long-ago baby kittens. None of her other furry family members, past or present, emanate that familiar, but for so many years forgotten, scent. Celia does not have any hay on her premises!

Celia told me that she was recently resting on her bed with Missy sleeping soundly right beside her head. "I wonder," Celia thought to herself; "is it really true? Are you that black-and-white childhood kitty?" A paw extended out and gently landed on the center of Celia's forehead.

∞

OF COURSE, this raises the question: If animals reincarnate, do we reincarnate, too? Yes. Divine Consciousness allows us to know, through channeling, that reincarnation does occur. The soul of a person or animal will often come back to the physical plane in a new body. It is hard to fully understand the broad implications of this because the human mind vibrates at a lower frequency than the soul does. In other words, as I understand it, the soul's migration may not be linear in a way that seems obvious to the mind.

In my channeling experience, human reincarnation has only been brought up a few times. The purpose was to identify past-life pain and trauma affecting the in-body person in their present incarnation, and then help them release it. I personally believe in reincarnation and find exploring the concept fascinating, and while other channelers will focus on revealing past lives, I am advised when I channel to put my attention on the current life of the person in front of me, along with their out-of-body loved ones, unless otherwise directed. Raising the issue of reincarnation opens a Pandora's box of questions that I do not feel qualified to answer. I simply stay in gratitude for what I am shown.

Clearly, consciousness itself is not limited to the linear perception of the physical brain; it is an extremely broad and continually expanding state of awareness that we may more fully comprehend when we are out of body, or when science advances its understanding of it. According to Walter Isaacson's biography of Einstein, Einstein discovered that "[t]ime cannot be absolutely defined, and there is an inseparable relation between time and signal velocity" Walter Isaacson, *Einstein, His Life and Universe* (Simon & Schuster: 2007, p. 123). Signal velocity is the speed at which a wave carries information, and how quickly a message can be communicated between two separated parties. Einstein, using measurements obtained on the physical plane, proved that "[t]here is no way to say that any two events are 'absolutely' or 'really' simultaneous. This is a simple insight, but also a radical one. It means there is no absolute time" (Isaacson, *Einstein*, p. 124).

Einstein channels in, "Imagine the expansive nature of time itself when signal velocity is measured within the nonbinding, higher frequency of my current place of existence."

In other words, signal velocity is not absolute and is a fluctuating variable on the physical plane. Einstein proposes that the broader and higher frequency of the spiritual plane would cause a greater fluctuation in the speed of informational travel, resulting in time being less of an absolute measurement.

We are capable of experiencing some semblance of this truth while we are in the physical body. Very often, at the end of channeling for someone, I am directed to ask the in-body person in front of me, "How much time do you think has gone by during our session?" The guess is consistently a small fraction of the actual time that has passed. I am then directed to point out that our perception of time moving more quickly during spiritual communication is a direct result of our rising, during channeling, to a higher level of vibration, the process that brings us closer to our loved ones who are out of body. As a result, with less of a vibrational frequency divide between us, we are able to literally feel their physical presence more easily. This wonderful higher-vibrational feeling, often referred to as the "zone," also attainable through the arts, nature, meditation, and prayer, is a spontaneous gift when our out-of-body loved ones are communicating. I believe it is the result of our shared intention and love.

This concept of time being a fluctuating variable has a lot of ramifications that are not so easily translated using traditional logic. If consciousness is not defined in linear terms, does that mean that you can channel an out-of-body person or animal who has passed and has gone on to reincarnate back into a physical body? My experience with channeling says Yes! Though most out-of-body humans report that they will wait, out of body, for loved ones to join them before deciding what to do next, there have been times when I will channel out-of-body consciousness that is capable of existing elsewhere, yet will manifest during channeling as who they were before they went on to another incarnation. It will be fun to apply the scientific formula to this equation once it is discovered.

ONE OF the greatest gifts that comes with animal companionship is the ability to be in the moment and allow ourselves to align with and enjoy their spontaneity. This is often a quick shortcut to that feeling of being in the "zone." When we acknowledge this two-way collaboration, both humans and animals are elevated and our energies are more closely aligned.

Sarah's Soul Cats

Our daughter, Sarah, has had cats in her life from the time she was born. In fact, her first sentence was "Yiyi bite!" Lily, a Himalayan cat, was apparently not enamored of Sarah's playful affection. Fortunately, for all the kitties that would join our family over the years, Sarah's feline love was undeterred.

Shadow, another Himalayan, loved Sarah's attention. Unfortunately, Shadow had ongoing health issues and passed when he was just two and a half years old. Over the years, other cats joined our family. Sarah loved them all and they all loved Sarah. Zoe, an American bobtail rescue, took to Sarah in a big way. Highly skittish, she found solace in Sarah's arms. When Sarah wasn't home, Zoe could be found on Sarah's bed in the company of her feline companion, Slash.

During this time, Sarah visited Israel and was astounded by the number of cats who independently roamed the streets. Of course Sarah loved them all, but one particular cat made it clear that he loved Sarah, too. He was the worse for wear, missing part of an ear, and scrappy because he had to be. He approached Sarah and crawled into her arms. They looked in each other's eyes and Sarah recognized her Shadow. Unable to take him home, she held him and hoped they would meet again.

Back home, Sarah took care of Zoe as she aged. When the time came, Sarah held her as she passed. Around this time, we could feel Shadow's presence and realized that he, as the Israeli kitty, had passed as well.

Once in a while, Sarah would ask me to channel her two beloved cats. They came in immediately. Sarah, who can also channel, could feel them. They communicated that they would both like to come back and share life with Sarah. The first time we channeled them, Shadow suggested that he come first, since he had passed so long ago. The next time we tuned in, a couple of months later, Shadow and Zoe were so happy together out of body that they had decided to come in as siblings. The male Shadow cat communicated that when the time came to be together again on the physical plane, he would approach Sarah first and she would recognize him. Both cats made it clear that they wanted to come in as very beautiful long-haired kittens. Before they could read my mind for my response, they reassured us that they would be rescues. They clearly knew that this was the path to our hearts and home.

About a year later, I saw a picture of a cat on social media. Homes were being sought for this mother cat and her babies, who were not in the picture. Though pretty, she did not have very long hair. But I did a double take as I realized that her energy resonated through the picture loud and clear. This felt like the one that had chosen my husband, Harry, many years ago. That sweet kitty, Lionel, had made it a practice to seek Harry out and gaze into his eyes. Then my logical mind took over. I told myself to let it go.

The next day, a dear friend called to say that her next-door neighbor was fostering a mama cat with three kittens. I wondered if it was the same cat I saw online; if so, she was being very diligent about making sure she found her way home to us! Of course, my husband and I went to see the cat family. The mama cat and the one I saw online were one and the same.

The mother cat, now known as Goldie, locked eyes with Harry and went right to him. She couldn't get close enough. Now, several years later, she behaves the same way whenever she is with him.

While Harry was drawn to this cat, I looked over at the three babies. Mama might not have had long hair, but Dad must have. Two of them exactly matched the channeled description of how Shadow and Zoe had planned to come in. The boy made eye contact first and came right over. His sister followed. I called Sarah to come see them. When she did, she quietly entered the room and sat on the floor. The boy, who shares Shadow's energy, went right to Sarah and crawled onto her lap, much like he did during his Israeli incarnation. The female kitten who shares Zoe's energy watched and waited patiently as Sarah and Shadow had their reunion. Then she also went straight to Sarah and nestled in. Named Basil and Penelope, these beautiful cats are now back in the physical, happily sharing our lives.

What happened to the third kitten? Sarah's friend, the daughter of the friend who told us about the cat family's plight, adopted him. I have the feeling that this friend and this kitty have also been together before.

I LOVE knowing that our out-of-body soul animals are able to create the circumstances that engage in-body people to support them, aligning us for a new life together on the physical plane. The help is out there, both guiding and networking for animals and people, to create the circumstances to bring and keep us together.

Clearly, that certain frequency is love!

Todd and His Dogs

Todd, the young man I met at the Compassionate Friends meeting who reassured his parents by letting them know that he's in Paradise, is helping his grandmother get ready to transition. I talked to his mom and he channeled in his perception of his grandmother's progress. His grandmother had recently celebrated her hundredth birthday, and she is not in a big hurry to go. Her body, on the other hand, is no longer able to hold her without a respirator and can no longer take in nourishment.

Todd's grandma told her daughter that she saw and heard dogs in the hospital hallway right outside her room. Todd's mom was there with her and knew that dogs, in the physical sense, had not been in the hallway, or anywhere nearby. Todd came right in to channel an explanation. His grandmother was perceiving the three golden retrievers he'd had when he was young, and who now accompany him on the spiritual plane. She was also aware of the presence of her own beloved dogs who had passed years ago.

Todd explained to his mother that his grandmother didn't want to go just yet. She was focusing her attention on her in-body loved ones. She was not ready for her out-of-body loved ones "to come and collect her." That's why his grandmother could hear the dogs "in the hallway."

Todd: Mom, she's getting ready, but she's a little scared. So it's easier for her to hear the dogs first. They're a segue to make it comfortable for her to hear and see everyone out here. They're letting her know that everything's okay. I'm here, too, and she's just beginning to realize that. Her mom is in the room and your dad. It's all okay. We'll all show her that she'll be able to see you. She'll have everyone out here but will also have access to everyone still there. The dogs are calming because she loves them, and they love her. So there's nothing scary about perceiving them, and then she'll know it's not scary to be with the rest of us!

TODD WANTS to remind me that the three dogs were an identifying factor when I channeled him for his parents for the first time at the Compassionate Friends meeting. The dogs helped introduce his parents to the reality of the spiritual plane. His mom and dad are able to live more fully and joyfully knowing that their son is no longer in pain, is with them, and is still enjoying the company of his three beloved dogs.

CHAPTER 13

Navigating Grief as Life Continues

It is inevitable that during the course of our lives we will experience the transition out of body of someone we love. And at various points, we may find ourselves back in the anger and guilt stage. This does not mean we are backtracking or losing ground. To accommodate the physical plane we are living in, we allow our vibration to lower as we process new or suppressed grief and pain.

The physical body and soul's wisdom allow for variations in our vibrational frequencies. Even if we know that our loved ones are fine out there, we shouldn't try to simply ignore our grief and pretend we're okay. Though knowing the spiritual truth gives us great comfort, we're still living in the physical body, and our arms long to hold our loved ones. We still wish to hear their voices. By recognizing our pain, processing, and releasing it, we can once again bring ourselves back into balance and high frequency, while maintaining our physical health and well-being.

Right now, as I write, I can't stop crying. Our dear friend's nineteen-year-old grandson passed yesterday after open-heart surgery. I grieve for his family and the now-aborted milestones and adventures they had hoped to share with him in the physical plane. I can channel and hear his grandmother, who passed before him; and I can reassure the family that he is fine, held, and loved. I know this is the truth, and yet I still cry.

We are here to learn that love is greater than pain, but sometimes the journey feels like walking a tightrope. We have proof that the big picture makes sense and hope that we will eventually understand why things are the way they are, but this truth is often unable to permeate the grief and sorrow. That's okay.

When this happens, we cry. We may be inconsolable. This grief is often exactly what the body, here on the physical plane, needs to feel in order to release our pain and sorrow. Though our society does not tend to give us much space or time for grief, it is imperative that we honor our pain and allow its release.

CONSCIOUSNESS IS the key.

My Mom and I

I've seen this so often in the course of my channeling: A person picks up a habit or trait from their passed loved one and carries it with them. Though it may not be healthy, it is a way to hold on to our loved one here on the physical plane. It can take the form of extra weight, physical symptoms, illness, and even opinions and biases.

I was shocked when it happened to me.

My mother had a rare form of cancer in her later years. It was not considered genetic. Surgery was successful and the cancer did not return for several years. When it did, surgery was not an option. She was too frail and the anesthesia too risky, but she did undergo seven weeks of radiation. This bought her a little more time here on the physical plane. When she passed a year and a half later, at age eighty-seven, I felt I had no right to grieve. After all, she had lived a long and happy life, and I knew that she was fine, with her loved ones, and able to see us. She was certainly more comfortable than she had been in the physical body. I tried to ignore how much I ached to hear her voice, how much I missed singing with her, and hugging her. I'd had her in my life longer than most people have their mothers, and we had always had a wonderful relationship. I knew I should just feel grateful. And besides, I'd be able to channel her.

A couple of years later, as I mentioned earlier, I was diagnosed with invasive breast cancer. This was not related to my mother's cancer. Since the cancer was particularly aggressive, after much soul-searching, in addition to natural healing modalities, I followed Western medicine protocol. I had several surgeries and radiation and was nearing the end of a year of chemotherapy.

Like most patients, I had many of the standard side effects. These were starting to ease up, as the last months of chemotherapy were less toxic. But just when it seemed like I was getting out of the woods, my entire body took a dive. I suddenly felt overwhelming pain and burning sensations in different parts of my body. My speech became slurred, and I could feel myself starting to leave my body, then getting pulled back in.

My husband called the oncologist. The medical consensus was that I was having a stroke and should come to the emergency room. When I heard this, I could hear my mother's response. She channeled in, "Don't go. If you pick up any bacteria or germs, it will kill you." Clearly, our out-of-body loved ones have a broad vantage point and are capable of perceiving and communicating information that can guide us in our times of need.

Thank God for my husband's faith in channeling. He was terrified, but we stayed put. I slowly improved, but it took a while to shake the burning sensations and pain. I saw the oncologist the following week and described my symptoms. He sat there quietly, and then said, "It's as if your body has a different kind of cancer and you had radiation on other parts of your body!" My husband put it together before I did. He looked at me and said, "Your body went through the side effects of your mother's treatment!"

Without being conscious of it, and without acknowledging and releasing the grief of my mother's passing, I carried a physical part of her. Of course, my mother, out of body, was not pleased with this and did everything she could to help me. I'm grateful for her counsel: there apparently was a staph infection going around the emergency room at the time I was directed to come in.

THIS WAS a personal and visceral lesson for me in allowing grief its physical process and not giving in to the logical mind's attempt to dismiss it. I'm so humbled and grateful to be allowed to channel, but I'm still in the physical body, subject to variations of frequency on many levels. I'm learning, just like everyone else. Having channeled access to higher vibrations does not exempt me from the necessary step of processing grief. Clearly, I tried that. But what I've learned was well worth the pain:

When you process and release emotional pain, as hard as that is, you're resetting your vibrational bar to go higher.

THERE'S NO beating the system. The laws of physics are at play here.

Heavier vibration brought about by grief is overwhelming and even scary when it sneaks up on you. Our soul's natural tendency is to want to rise to a more comfortable vibrational frequency. But allowing your grief to follow its course will help restore your balance. And doing so will help you recognize once again your true nature as a spiritual being residing in a physical body.

An interesting concept was recently channeled in that answered some of my long-standing questions. I had wondered why so many movies and books directly marketed to young children are filled with heartbreaking loss. A parent may be killed as the movie opens, or maybe the heroic dog meets an untimely end. The grimness of *Grimm's Fairy Tales* was not lost on me.

Guides recently reported, through channeling, that this heartbreaking fiction regularly offered to children is not intended to be sadistic. In fact, it's quite the opposite. I was informed that some writers and animators are actually guided to create these morbid scenarios. Why? Our society is not comfortable with expressions of grief and pain. So many people for whom I have channeled experienced the passing of a parent or sibling when they were young. Often, they are not given sufficient information about what happened, even though their world has dramatically changed.

Children are intuitive and comprehend when adults are uncomfortable. As a result, many children stop asking questions in an effort to not upset the very people who can help them. As these children tiptoe around other people's pain and grief, they end up sublimating their own. For optimal emotional and physical health, this grief needs to be released in a way that the child perceives to be appropriate and acceptable.

Watching a movie in which a parent is distant or evil, or in which a loving parent dies, triggers a child's emotions and can be the necessary catalyst to shake loose some of that bottled-up grief and pain. The child is given the space to cry and be upset, but it is all safe and socially acceptable, and centered around a topic or story that is not as personal as the devastating loss the child may be dealing with in real life. Many adults will not feel threatened by a display of emotion if the cause is neatly packaged and presented.

I can't tell you how often out-of-body loved ones channel in to tell their in-body loved ones that pent-up grief is not healthy and needs to be released. They assign homework that their loved ones can do on the physical plane to relieve the emotional pain. And their frequent prescription for both adults and children: watch a children's movie that will help touch the nerve that will release the tears. Even if this catalyst is not directly related to one's own personal tragedy, the release of pent-up grief is healthy and will help the physical body return to a more comfortable higher vibration. A child who is taught to repress emotion becomes an adult who represses emotion. And there is the added danger that we might become so accustomed to the pain and grief that we no longer realize it is even there. This pain may then have the opportunity to become the silent repressor of our energetic frequency, as well as our health.

Think about it. If a child is dealing with horrific loss, it may be too deep and personal to express, especially around adults who are traumatized themselves. In watching or reading a tragic tale, the child maintains autonomy and may not be judged for crying. There is no need to feel guilty about triggering someone else's pain by bringing up a loss that the child may perceive as a taboo subject. And of course a sad film that triggers tears is helpful for adults, too.

Another suggestion from our out-of-body loved ones to help us relieve suppressed grief: an animal friend. Almost any animal pal will do, but most dogs are specifically wired to be empaths, as are many cats, horses, and other animals. They have the expanded emotional sensory perception and presence to help us stabilize our moods and vibrational frequencies. We know that petting an animal usually results in lowering blood pressure and stress. If we take it just a step further, we realize that an animal is the perfect companion for a child who needs to talk and release tears. The child has the opportunity to emote without taking the gamble of upsetting others. There is no need to suppress the truth, as an animal companion can tell no tales.

Of course, it is best for everyone to share and release grief in a timely manner. Thankfully, the world seems to be becoming a more conscious and fertile place for processing truth and trauma. But animals will always remain a sweet and perfect catalyst because their instinct may allow them to be tuned in to our pain more efficiently than we allow ourselves to be. This realization could help clear animal shelters as we go adopt potential healers.

Furthermore, when we share our pain with others, scary as that may be, we are clearing a path for them as well. They may need the catalyst of us sharing our pain to help them release their own.

We're in this life together. Companionship, emotional intimacy, and camaraderie are all sure ways to raise and maintain high-vibrational frequency.

Most people do not intend to isolate themselves from others in their grief, and they do not knowingly encourage its suppression. It is often our own empathic response to others that leads us to not share, just like the children who learn to hold back their emotions. When we know others are suffering along with us, we may not want to add to their grief by sharing our own. But while the isolation and repression of pain and grief may begin with good intentions, bringing this pattern to consciousness can help all of us as it leads us to share and release our pain in the most helpful and appropriate manner.

CHAPTER 14

Keeping the Door Open: Spiritual Access in Everyday Life

A s we consciously choose to pay attention to the moment we are in, and incorporate more and more of the high-frequency magnificence available on the physical plane, something happens. Remember the old adage to stop and smell the roses? There is a lot of wisdom in that recommendation. Guides advise us to attune our senses to fully appreciate what surrounds us. When we are present to enjoy the hug, the laughter, the music, nature's splendor, and other enjoyable earth offerings, our frequency gets used to residing at a higher-vibrational level. Throwing in some gratitude for the things we appreciate multiplies the effect. This, of course, does not mean being in denial about what causes us pain. But it does mean allowing ourselves to receive from loved ones, as well as from the earth's physical bounty. In addition, this process brings us more awareness of the visits and signs from those residing on the spiritual plane.

Lifting our sprits opens us up to the spiritual!

Spontaneous Channeling

You're driving along and hear a conversation with your out-of-body loved one in your head. You hear, you answer, and back and forth it goes. Sometimes it's memory and sometimes it's wishful thinking. But often it's not! You're having a real conversation. You are channeling!

Time and time again, during a channeling session, the out-of-body loved one comes through and recounts such a conversation, often line by line. The out-of-body loved one reassures the person here that the conversation was not a figment of their imagination. As you know, I believe that all of us have the ability to channel. It is so gratifying to witness a person come to the conscious realization that they are not just capable of channeling, they have been actively doing it! Do you know who's the first to be aware of your expanding perception? Your out-of-body loved ones! They are learning along with us, clandestinely teaching us as they are also longing to comfort and reassure us.

There are a couple of things to remember. If you are actively grieving, your vibration is lower. This is to be expected, as you need to allow your physical self to mourn the physical loss. Don't despair if your channeling efforts are not bringing results as quickly as you'd like. Try not to think too hard about it. Even though the mind is having the conversation, the brain is not in charge. Usually this type of spontaneous channeling is happening when your thinking is otherwise occupied—for example, when you are driving, or performing physical tasks during which you can be somewhat on autopilot. Your vibrational frequency is rising, maybe as a result of your out-of-body loved one's intention, or maybe your

own. If you're not sure which, it's safe to assume that it's a mutual
desire, and that reciprocal love, in and of itself, raises the frequency.

You Felt Me

Carla's son Kyle had passed three years before she came to me for
a session. He had been alone in the car when he fell asleep at the
wheel. After relating the circumstances of his physical passing, his
gratitude that no one else was hurt, and the details of the life he'd
had on the physical plane, he congratulated his mother on her ability to pick up his thoughts and act on them.

KYLE (LAUGHING): So, you got some sneakers last week!

CARLA: What!? How do you know that?

KYLE (CONTINUING TO LAUGH): Mom, I was right there! I'll
prove it to you! You were down to two pairs. One pair was white
with a purple stripe. The other ones were blue.

CARLA: That's right! That's exactly right! I don't believe this is
happening!

KYLE: You bought the blue ones!

CARLA: I did!

KYLE: You know why?

CARLA: Oh my God! [Stops for a moment to breathe.] Oh my
God!

KYLE: Right! You remember.

CARLA: I went back and forth so many times and kept trying
them both on. Whenever I put on the blue ones, I just got the
weirdest feeling, like everything is fine. Don't worry about any-

thing. So I bought them. In a weird way, when I put them on, or just look at them, they make me happy.

KYLE: Mom, you felt me! It was me! I like those blue sneakers. Whenever you put them on, I hugged you.

CARLA: I felt him! I didn't know it, but I felt him!

KYLE: I've been hugging you all along. Sometimes, when I did, you would start to cry. I know you would just say, "I'm having one of those moments!" Well, sometimes, I just needed to hug you, and you didn't know why you got all emotional. Other times, when you were emotional, I thought you needed an extra hug. It kind of goes back and forth. You know why?

CARLA: Why?

KYLE: Because I'm right there. And because I can. And, because I love you.

CARLA: This is unbelievable! I have to think about everything in a new way. This makes me so happy!

KYLE: Hey, Mom, it makes me really happy that you know. I'll keep doing it!

CARLA: Thank you, Kyle! I love you so much.

KYLE: Well, obviously I love you, too, Mom. I still do!"

IT'S ALWAYS a sweet reminder of the big picture when an out-of-body loved one observes and channels in the specific reactions of their in-body loved ones, in response to their presence and hugs. The high percentage of channeling sessions that reveal this level of spontaneous communication can be viewed as a kind of psychic X-ray that exposes the reality that this is happening all the time!

I have heard from clients and have observed with my own family and friends that when attention is brought to this once-unconscious phenomenon (as I write this, a group of out-of-body children are surrounding me and they want to complete the sentence): the fun and games can really begin!

Adam

Adam's grandmother and my mom were friends since second grade. I met Adam twenty years ago when he moved to California from Massachusetts, shortly after we did. His dream was to write and direct horror movies. With unwavering diligence and plenty of talent, he did just that. Adam is a sweet guy and we have stayed in touch, even though I admit that horror and gore are not my genres of choice.

Over the years, we would channel in the wise counsel of Adam's grandfather when there were questions about health and family matters. I was surprised, as it felt out of character, when Adam called one day sounding absolutely terrified. What he described sounded more like one of his movie scripts as opposed to his normal life.

ADAM: You have to get over here—there's a ghost in my apartment! Other people in the building have seen him. I know he's in here! He keeps moving things around.

My husband and I went right over to Adam's place to see what was going on. As soon as we entered, I could feel the presence of a young boy, maybe nine or ten years old. He happily and quite innocently channeled in that he loved coming to Adam's place because Adam had the best toys! Adam did indeed have quite the treasure trove of movie-related models and gadgets, the kind of stuff that a kid that age would find appealing. I explained to the boy that Adam was pretty frightened by his ability to move things around and leave his belongings in disarray. The boy acknowledged that he was beginning to realize this. He made it clear that his intention was just to play. He told us a little about his situation and family. He had passed from illness several years before, and though he liked to spend time with his in-body family, who lived nearby, and his out-of-body grandparents, he was intrigued when he happened to chance upon Adam and saw him carrying a few toys. So he came in and played with them. Not wanting to cause further worry, the boy moved on and Adam's toy collection stayed put.

A year or so later, I received another frightened call from Adam. For the past few nights, he could feel his blanket slowly being pulled down, as if someone was at the foot of the bed, pulling on it. I tuned in and asked what was going on. Adam's protective and loving grandfather came right in. He laughed and said that there was no cause for alarm.

Suddenly, the room filled with many out-of-body people. The group was composed of mostly adolescent males, with several exceptions. They were friendly and nonthreatening. They communicated that they loved Adam's movies! Yes, they liked the horror genre! And yes, they have access to movies and other earthly offerings. They will watch movies together with friends they have met since going out of body, or they will accompany their in-body family or friends when they go to the movies.

This group happened to love the terror and the rush that the movies provided. So they had gotten together as a group to say thank you—their goal had been nothing more than to return the favor, by supplying Adam with a good scare! Adam let them know, in no uncertain terms, that they had more than accomplished their mission. Could they please stop?

Adam's visitors shed light on the varied and broad range of intentions of those who are out of body. When they understood the depth of Adam's terror, they were able to have an empathic response and willingly decided to cease and desist. Clearly, their concern for Adam's well-being overrode the fun they were having. Though Adam was scared, he could acknowledge the humor in the high jinks. They are over my shoulder as I write this, and they want you to know that they were just having fun.

∞

IT IS important to feel safe as you become comfortable with and adept at channeling. How you choose to implement your expanding abilities is up to you. When you ask for protection, and then state your intention, you let Divine Consciousness know what works for you. Remember, I didn't have a filter until I asked for one. I only stopped seeing upsetting things that I had no control over when I asked Divine Consciousness to help me. Putting protection around yourself is essential. If your intention is to only have interactions with specific out-of-body people, ask for that. If you would like to be of service to others, let Divine Consciousness know. When you are vibrating at a high frequency and willing to be a communication conduit, out-of-body people, in their quest to help in-body loved ones, may employ you to get a message across.

It Will Be Okay!

I was in the middle of purchasing a faucet at a large home improvement store when someone caught my attention. An out-of-body woman was standing directly behind the middle-aged in-body female cashier.

OUT-OF-BODY WOMAN: Please, this is my daughter. Tell her I'm here with her.

ME (THANKFUL THAT THERE WAS NO ONE IN LINE BEHIND ME): Listen, I can see people who have passed, and your mom is with you. She wants you to know that.

CASHIER (I HAD HER FULL ATTENTION): Oh my God! I've been asking her if she's with me!

OUT-OF-BODY WOMAN: You had the biopsy. I know about it, and you're going to be okay. There's a little something going on. You'll need a bit of medical intervention, but you'll be all right. You'll survive.

CASHIER: She's with me? She knows! I'm so scared.

OUT OF BODY WOMAN: I know! I'm with you and you'll be fine.

CASHIER: Oh my God, thank you so much! Thank you! That's just what I needed to know. Can I give you a discount on the faucet? Let me see what I can do.

ME (LAUGHING): Thank you, but not necessary. We're bosom buddies! I've been through it, too.

The cashier came out from behind the counter to give me a hug.

AFTER THIS encounter I commented to Harry that it always amazes me that spontaneous encounters like this one are met with eagerness and enthusiasm. I then heard out-of-body laughter. Higher-level guides channeled in: "We only send you to the people who are open and able to receive the message."

This is nice to hear. While I always choose to relay messages that I receive, it is comforting to know that I don't have to worry about someone getting irate, upset, or even scared. The protection I use includes asking to be an instrument for healing as Divine Consciousness sees fit. Of course, it makes sense that with this high intention, all spontaneous channeling encounters are good for everyone involved.

Catalysts for Spontaneous Channeling

Our natural instinct is to be drawn to high-vibrational beauty, art, and people. Celia, Jack's mom, often uses the phrase "Follow the pleasure." Whether Jack calls her attention to heart-shaped rocks or manifests his profile in a ribbon of light, which he has done, he is filling her heart with joy. Her adage to follow the pleasure is the mind's recognition of the soul's desire to fill her whole being with joy. Many of her mother-and-son encounters take place in the forest, so Celia is sure to walk her big dog, Sabrina, there on a regular basis.

The forest itself is high vibration, as are Sabrina's happy hound dog explorations. Does this setting guarantee an out-of-body manifestation? Not always, but setting the scene for high-vibration interactions is an invitation. Our out-of-body loved ones are aware of our intention. If we lay the groundwork, it is that much easier for them to collaborate with us, as we are raising our vibrational field more closely to theirs.

It is channeled in that the laws of physics support this theory. In other words, when we consciously choose to raise our vibration to increase our joy, and as a means of welcoming our out-of-body loved ones' communications, the nature of our preparation further raises the vibration. As a result, our out-of-body loved ones are happy. Along with knowing that we are consciously acknowledging them and inviting them in, they see us actively taking steps to take good care of ourselves by embracing the joy and beauty of the physical world.

Many out-of-body people, like Isabel, who was struck by a car and passed before her mother could reach her, are sometimes frustrated by their inability to take care of us more actively. Many of us have experienced the frustration of wishing our out-of-body loved ones could help us on the physical plane while we process the grief of their loss. We may be grieving for a parent, for example, and miss them all the more since that parent would ordinarily have been the person who would support us through our grief. Parents realize that they will not be physically present when their child mourns them, though their child, of course, needs them more than ever now, as they learn to negotiate a physical world that previously did not exist without their parent. Imagine the parents' joy, then, when their child sets the table for high-frequency encounters. The preparation itself is what the parent would ask the child to do for the child's own healing. Our good intentions magnify the vibration and healing for all.

Start paying attention, if you haven't already, to the energies that surround you. You have a choice. You can choose to surround yourself with clear and uplifting people, media, and environments. When I had cancer, I found I could not be subjected to movies, television, or music that I found violent or destructive. We learn through cause and effect how watching the news before bed affects our sleep. Choosing uplifting and inspiring input helps in myriad ways to provide an ever-expanding opportunity to heal.

Then, of course, there is the motivation for collaboration. Feeling better leads to our being more open and better able to receive our out-of-body loved one's messages.

A few years ago, I went to a movie with Celia about opening up to the spiritual world. Shortly after it started, I became aware of Jack's presence. He was with us. At this point, my perceiving his presence was not unusual. What did surprise me was this: at the end of the movie, I could easily see that the out-of-body people far outnumbered the in-body moviegoers! As we rose to leave, Jack told me that these out-of-body people enjoyed the movie, but their true motivation was to take advantage of the raised vibration the subject matter brought to their loved ones on the physical plane. "They're more open to hearing us," Jack explained. Those out-of-body people will be in the car going home with their in-body people and trying out their own developing skills at getting communication through.

So, pay attention to the vibrational levels around you and make choices with consciousness. This doesn't mean that you need to leave your favorite storytelling genres behind. Like Adam, you just might find that what you're passionate about may be entertaining to out-of-body as well as in-body people. That, in and of itself, can be uplifting.

How to Raise Your Vibrational Level:

Right now, reading this, you're doing it!
   Remember that every breath is natural mouth-to-mouth resuscitation from Divine Consciousness.
   Just thinking about this raised your vibration.

Allow yourself to appreciate the beauty around you . . . you are part of that beauty.
   Think about:

- People you love
- Animals you love
- Music you love
- Places you love

   All the sweetness that brings you joy.
   And you're doing it!

Your intention to raise your vibration is already raising it. Whether by:

- Thinking about it
- Reading about it
- Talking about it, which raises it even higher

Don't "work" too hard. Don't worry about your progress.

- You own this.
- It is your birthright.
- Share with others. We are all catalysts for each other's expansion.

   We are all in this together.

Mom's Reassurance

I had been recently diagnosed with cancer, and the surgeon felt it was her duty to inform me that the prognosis was grim. If you or a loved one has been through this, then you know the extensive medical testing that goes with the territory. My friend Enid took me to many of these appointments, and today was no exception. I was pressed into a machine where I felt like the innards of a metal sandwich. After what seemed like a very long time, I was told that there was a suspicious area and that more time in the claustrophobic machine was needed. Thankfully, at the end of the test, the kind medical technician told me that though he was not supposed to say anything to me about the exams, the shadows showing up on the screen might just be scar tissue from old injuries, as opposed to additional cancer sites.

Somewhat relieved, Enid and I took the elevator to the hospital lobby, deliberating over where to go to lunch. Though my mind may have thought it was able to carry the stress, my body told its truth as my knees buckled and I hit the floor. With help, I was ushered over to the lobby's seating area to catch my breath.

This particular hospital offered staff and patients a treat. A pianist, who was blind, volunteered there a couple of times a week. As she performed, I recalled how comforted I'd been by her music several years earlier, when I would visit my mother after her cancer surgery. As I sat and reminisced, I could feel my mother hug me.

Mom: Watch! Watch the piano player!

The pianist finished playing, sat back with her eyes closed, and folded her hands in her lap.

MOM: She's downloading the song I'm asking her to play for you!

After a moment or two, the woman leaned toward the piano and started to play "Here, There and Everywhere." This was my mother's favorite Beatles song, the one I sang to her over and over as she got ready to pass!

I projected my thanks to Divine Consciousness, my mother, and the perceptive piano player for this precious gift. I realized that a terrifying experience had paved the way for my mother to let me know she was still with me "here, there, and everywhere."

Harry's Dad

Our older son's bar mitzvah was a joyful day filled with love, family, and friends. Both grandmothers were physically present; both grandfathers had passed years before. We were happily exhausted at the end of the day. The house was finally quiet, the kids asleep. Harry was in bed, sitting up, and I continued to share with him the highlights of the day as I got ready to join him. I turned to look at Harry as I was talking and saw that he was wide awake, staring at the foot of the bed. Whatever it was had his full attention. I did not turn to see what he was looking at. I instinctively felt that what he was seeing was meant for him.

A moment passed.

Harry then turned to me, his face aglow. That is the only way I can describe it. With eyes and heart wide with wonder, he shared his experience. He had seen gold light, and in the center of that light stood his father, dressed in a suit and wearing a tallit, the traditional Jewish prayer shawl. He held his hand out to Harry as if to shake hands. His face was beaming with joy.

Harry, who has grown accustomed to my perceptions, could not recall ever having had an experience of this nature. He was so excited as he described what he had seen. His father's presence on that particular day was a gift. His timing and how he presented himself fully acknowledged the significance of the day. Harry could feel the love and pride emanating from his father.

As I write this and reminisce about what a sacred gift Harry's father gave him, I hear that it was in response to a sacred gift that he and other out-of-body loved ones were themselves given that day.

Many years before, after they were liberated from the German concentration camps, Harry's parents found that they were the only survivors of their families.

"Imagine," Harry's dad is channeling in, "all of the simchas [happy occasions] we did not have, all the lives cut short, the children who did not live to celebrate their milestones. All these years later, we gather and rejoice together with you. Our hearts are filled as we celebrate together."

I KNOW it took a lot of energy for Harry's father to manifest so strongly. And at this moment, his father is channeling in an interesting concept that I have never thought of before.

"When you celebrate, when you dance and sing, when you express gratitude, we, in spirit, who celebrate with you, are energized and filled with joy!"

I am hearing that this truth permeates all religions and celebrations that sanctify life and gratitude.

I see crowds of out-of-body celebrants at Christmas parties, Nowruz (Persian New Year) parties, baby namings, brises, christenings, weddings, and funerals. When there is a gathering of love and thankfulness, they gather with us. Though rituals may vary, the light and love coming through from the spiritual plane is universal, amplifying the joy and expanding the love, whether we are conscious of it or not.

So then, why not actively invite them to join the festivities? Acknowledging our out-of-body loved ones' continued involvement makes them happy, and reminds us that they love to share our joy.

Dream Visits

It is natural for us, when we are missing loved ones, to ask them to come visit in a dream. I have learned through channeling that our loved ones are often trying to accommodate us, though the results may not be immediate. They remind us that this is a new venture for them, as well as for us. During channeled sessions, out-of-body loved ones will corroborate their in-body loved ones' experiences.

"You could feel me! You woke up thinking it was real. It was!"

"Remember that dream? I was wearing my favorite blue shirt and you hugged me. That was not a dream, that really happened."

"I got through twice! You had two dreams, and we talked, but you couldn't remember what I said when you woke up. That's okay. I'm just learning how to do it, too."

Out-of-body people have channeled in and described their loved ones' dreams so often, and accurately, that there can be no doubt of their authenticity. Our out-of-body loved ones report that the sleep state is high vibration and conducive to real-time visits. Of course, dreams can take many forms and serve many purposes, as Freud and others have taught us. But if you wake up with the feeling that you have viscerally experienced something and the feeling remains vivid, it was most likely a real exchange with your loved one.

If you'd like to try to communicate with loved ones in a dream, set aside some time before you go to sleep. Be patient. Ask for protection. Then, state your intention. You may be more comfortable asking that everything that comes in be for healing purposes. Specify and invite the person, or people, you would like to communicate with. It might take time for your own vibrational level to adjust while grieving. Don't despair if you cannot remember any details other than the presence or touch of your loved ones. Maybe that's all they can do right now, and all you need.

But don't try to sleep your life away. Remember, embracing the physical world with joy raises the vibration and is a catalyst for all energetic exchanges. Still, before you go to sleep, why not invite them in as you send them love.

Manifestations

Though I know that our out-of-body loved ones are capable of getting our attention, and that they play with high-frequency energy that resonates closely with their own vibration, still, I have to admit that sometimes I am completely taken aback by their tenacity as well as their abilities. I can't explain how they do what they do, but I have witnessed it.

A solid item might shift position, or behave in an unexpected way. Todd's parents, whom I met when I went with Alan's mother, Fay, to a Compassionate Friends meeting, brought me a beautiful orchid when I was starting cancer treatment. Todd was present when they presented this gift and channeled in that he would see to it that the orchid would bloom and not go dormant until I was done with the roughest part of treatment. That orchid bloomed for thirteen months! The last flower held on until three weeks after my last infusion. I was amazed at Todd's attention to detail. Chemo was every three weeks, so the last bloom fell off after the last treatment had run its course.

While I'm always amazed at the many ways our out-of-body loved ones affect the physical world, my dad managed to do something that even I find incredible.

My Dad's Vest

My mother was my father's primary caretaker for the last few years of his life. Eventually his health required a lot more care than she could provide. Following his last stay in the hospital, he was discharged to a skilled nursing facility. Though his dementia was aggravated by the surgery he had recently gone through, he appeared to be getting stronger. He went into the nursing facility on a Tuesday. My mother and a friend sat with me as I wrote his name in marker on the labels of his clothes.

Then, as I mentioned earlier, on the following Friday, during our visit, he told me to come the next day at one o'clock. He passed on Saturday at noon. Later, my mother asked the facility coordinator for my father's personal items. We were told that his things were all gone. Other patients had apparently wandered into his room and taken what they liked, a practice I later learned was not uncommon. There had been nothing there of great monetary value—just some clothes, an electric shaver, and a framed family picture.

A few months later, my mom was packing up my father's things for donation. His dresser was now completely empty. My mother asked if there were any items I would like to keep. My dad's signature outfits in those days included a sweater vest that would match his pants. I told my mom that I would like to keep his favorite one, a cranberry-and-white plaid. Then we realized that it was gone—it had been one of the items that had gone missing in the nursing home. I took his key case instead. I liked the idea of having a well-worn item that he'd carried with him for years.

That was that, until a few days later, when my mother opened my father's empty dresser drawer. She could not believe her eyes. There, folded neatly, by itself, was my father's cranberry-and-white sweater vest! I have it to this day. Once in a while, I take it out and thank my dad. It's good to be reminded that something can happen that completely challenges my preconceived idea of reality.

ALBERT EINSTEIN said that there are two ways to live your life. One, as though nothing is a miracle, the other as though everything is.

Ashley—Iridescence

It was Ashley's birthday and her friend had just given her a new puppy. They were about to go into the pet supply store to buy the food and other items they needed when the puppy got loose and darted into the parking lot. Ashley dashed after her and was struck down by an oncoming truck. Though help came quickly, she passed before it arrived.

Several years before this happened, Ashley's parents, Michele and Angus, had brought Ashley along with them for a channeling session. A friend of Ashley's, who had become close to the family, had recently passed. Ashley was fascinated by the concept of channeling and wanted to know as much as she could about the process. I'm sure that her curiosity and desire to learn how her friend could communicate are serving her now as she guides her parents through the grieving process.

The first time Ashley channeled to her parents, she wanted to assure them that even though they were not particularly fond of the friend who had given her the puppy and who was there when she transitioned out of body, her death was still an accident and the friend had been traumatized. She did not want her parents to be mired in anger, though she certainly understood that it was natural to initially blame the person who seemed to have caused the situation. She understands her parents' point that the friendship was not the healthiest, but that didn't mean that the friend was guilty of anything more. She preferred that her parents let go of the "if it weren't for that person" scenario and embrace the fact that if Ashley was going to leave the physical plane, she did it while trying to save an animal. Her parents agreed that Ashley's take on things reflected her kind and generous nature.

Michele and Angus continue to talk to, and encourage, their daughter. They did not have to wait long before very specific Ashley-style manifestations started to happen. Always an artistic child, Ashley loves "iridescence" and considers it her favorite color. I use the present tense because clearly Ashley's preference has not changed. The first time her parents noted a sign from Ashley was when they found a big sheet of iridescent cellophane tucked under the windshield wipers of their car. Certainly this was strange, but it could have been a random act. That idea was shelved when they realized that things were just getting started. Ashley's parents started finding strands of iridescent ribbon quite regularly in the most unlikely places. Recently, when we met, Michele pulled out a plastic bag filled with glistening strands! She was so excited to share that this was just a fraction of what they have received.

Angus is determined that he and Michele continue to be the upbeat and optimistic people that Ashley loves. Smiling through her tears, Michele shared with me all the many ways that the mother-daughter bond continues.

MICHELE: It's hard when I think about all the milestones we anticipated. We won't get to watch her face as she gets married, and we won't get to witness her becoming a mother, as we'd always hoped. But we can still help her. I talk to her every day. She is still such a big part of our lives. She's still with us. Though this isn't what we envisioned, there are gifts. [Michele held up the bag of ribbons.] These are showing up in the craziest places. I know it's Ashley letting us know she is with us.

. . .

MICHELE AND Angus shared with me that one of Ashley's former boyfriends and his family have made it a point to include them in family gatherings. I could hear Ashley's answer before her mother could finish the question.

ASHLEY: Yes! He's really important to me, and I think he was "the guy." So I pushed the idea, so that he would realize that it's really good for you to be included with his family. It's good for everybody, him too!

MICHELE: It's so comfortable! This young man and his family are happy to talk about Ashley. So many people avoid us or won't mention her name. I get it, it's scary for them.

ANGUS: People act like it's contagious. I understand. I don't hold it against them.

ASHLEY: People don't know what to say or do. They look at me as being part of the past. They don't understand that we're together and I'm still part of your life. They don't experience that reality. So they're coming at it from their perspective only and that makes it scary for them. I'm so happy you're telling people the truth! You talk to people and share what's real. You have to know how much that helps people. When you were talking to those people whose son passed and telling about me bringing you signs, their son was standing right next to me! He was so happy! Now it will be easier for him to get through to his family! They're open and looking for signs now, too. I have it easy because you're just so aligned with me. You see what I'm doing.

MICHELE: Oh, I can feel her all the time! I know it's her!

ASHLEY: And that helps me so much. I felt so bad that everyone was so sad. I didn't want to make anyone unhappy. But together we're helping each other and other people, too. When you get here, a long time from now, we'll be proud of each other!

And Dad, I know you're still angry about that friend and everything that happened.

ANGUS NODDED his head in agreement.

ASHLEY: I think you need to go in a room by yourself and scream a few times to let it out. I get it, but I don't want you to be mad forever. It's not good for you. I love you and I love being with you. I'll keep learning here, I promise, and we can do this.

Michelle and Angus continue to find strands of iridescent ribbon. They recently installed a security camera at their front door, Angus told me in an email. "We have not had any security issues. However, Ashley is manifesting ribbons in front of the camera." Included in the email is a video, taken in the evening. The clarity of the iridescent ribbon is startling as it floats and waves brightly against the contrast of the night's sky.

Automatic Writing

Matteo, who passed at age fourteen and wanted to be a surgeon, was eager to learn more about medicine. His mom, Rachelle, still encourages him to continue his studies. In an effort to sharpen her proficiency to "hear" her son's responses, she picked up a pen and asked Matteo if he would like to write through her. Rachelle is right-handed. She had an impulse to switch hands and write with her left, something she had never done before. She did not have as much control over her writing this way and thought that it would be easier for Matteo to guide her. It took a little practice, but before long, the writing was flowing. The style of the wording was definitely her son's, but she was also amazed when she realized that what she had written completely matched Matteo's own handwriting!

How to Sharpen the Tools in Your Energetic Toolbox

Children are born with spiritual access and memory. How can we help them maintain the ability to tap into this expansive and helpful resource? It is important to realize that when we enter the world as babies, we are both distracted by and enchanted with the physical world. It makes sense to keep our main focus on the in-body people around us and not distance ourselves from the physical beauty as well as the challenges around us. As we know, lifting our vibration to expand our access to the spiritual plane is strengthened as a result of embracing the beauty and joy of the physical plane. So it is no surprise that playfulness on the physical plane is a strong catalyst for lifting our vibration. When I was a child, my mother and I had a little game. She would whisper the name of a popular song to me, and I would then quietly focus on it. Invariably, my brother, Mark, who was in another room, would start humming or whistling that exact tune. We got a kick out of it every time. At that age, I welcomed safe playful psychic expansion.

Because it was just a game, with no agenda other than delighting in our connectedness, it normalized the idea of telepathy for me and my brother. I recently asked Mark if he considered himself to be a spiritual conduit. He said he does not. He might believe that, but I do not. All people have the capacity to pick up our loved ones' vibrations. It is common knowledge that many siblings, especially twins, are able to sense each other's pain or fear. This is true for many parents and children, and of course for many other deep and close relationships. It makes sense if you realize that the energy of our vibrational frequency is directed by much more than our thoughts. Our heart, digestive tract, pituitary gland, and countless other human systems function without our conscious directions. Our energetic system works the same way. We are constantly receiving energetic and vibrational information, integrating it, and responding to it without the conscious mind perceiving the entire operation. I think this is how it works for Mark. When I am about to call him, the phone will usually ring, and there he is. We'll often say the same thing at the same time. I believe that such strong intuition is second nature for him and he doesn't know he is doing it.

Think about it.

- I had a bad feeling and knew not to go. I didn't know why, but look what happened.
- I could feel that person wasn't being honest before a word was said.
- I was just thinking about them when they called.
- I had a hunch and went to the doctor. Thank God I did.
- I had a feeling something was going on with you!

It all comes down to intention. When we care about each other's well-being, our natural ability to pick up each other's frequency is expanded.

If you would like to expand and sharpen energetic access, be playful. Joy is high-vibration. By yourself, or with loved ones whom you trust, ask for protection and then set your intention. The goal is not manipulation, it is expansion. My mother and I were not trying to control my brother's thoughts. The purpose was to play with him. The game would make us all laugh, as we learned about strengthening energetic bonds. We didn't know we were doing that at the time. We just thought it was cool.

When our daughter was four or five, she came up with a game. She would close her eyes and have me choose a crayon to put in her hands. She would focus and feel it with her eyes still closed. She would then, accurately, tell me the color. She said that she could "feel" the color. This game, of her own design, supported and helped her develop abilities that we did not perceive at that time. As an adult, she can look around the room and tell us the color of each person's energetic field. She says she doesn't physically see the color; instead, she feels it. I can then look around the room and confirm with my physical vision that she is correct. I realize now that the game she invented supported her own individual mode of accessing energetic information.

Most important, when I played these games with my mother and daughter, no one looked at what we were doing and told us it was impossible.

Think of the many times you feel something or think of something and then have confirmation that you were "tuning in." I believe it happens to all of us. Bringing this psychic ability to consciousness can be great fun. And fun is the key. We may be prone to exercising our instincts around accidents and trauma, as the stakes and energy are high and the gift feels most meaningful. But, in ordinary circumstances, it is best to stay light and not get bogged down in trying too hard or intellectualizing your efforts. That type of thinking will lower the vibration and inhibit the ability you are looking to expand.

Part of the reason our games worked is because there was no preconceived idea of how they should go. Were they directed by our subconscious or Divine Consciousness in order to hone our specific abilities? Maybe. That's a fun thought that I believe is true. So much of what we are drawn to can broaden our horizons in ways we are not conscious of.

This happened in a big way for my own personal growth, but I did not realize it until much later.

In graduate school, I studied theater, specializing in acting. I felt compelled to do this even though I did not have the drive to pursue an acting career. Method acting was in vogue at that time, and we were trained in Lee Strasberg's techniques. Strasberg emphasized that the actor must be a blank slate in order to truly take on someone else's persona, and to be truly blank, it was necessary to release all of the tension we held. We were taught through exercises that have been described as similar to meditation practices.

I couldn't get enough of these acting classes. The focus was on emotion and authenticity. I resonated with the primary direction given: "Get out of the way and let the character come through you!"

More than twenty years later, I was driving alone when I had a spontaneous revelation. I had to pull the car over, I was laughing so hard. It dawned on me that all of that acting training was precisely what I needed to prepare me for a career in channeling! I was taught to use myself as an instrument, allowing someone else to come through! As I sat there laughing, I realized that guides were laughing with me. "You knew this all along!" I blurted out. I felt a "wave" as guides hugged me. I channeled in: "Yes, you took our direction to prepare yourself for what you now do. We were waiting for you to make the connection!" I continued to laugh with them, until I cried with gratitude.

I remember Alfred Sensenbach, a bigwig in the Emerson theater department, cornering me in a hallway. "When are you going to get serious?" he asked me. Though my grades were stellar because I loved the material, it was probably obvious that I lacked the ambition and thick skin necessary to successfully pursue an acting career. I gleefully replied, "Never!" He smiled, shook his head, and walked away.

It wasn't until so many years later that I understood that my response to Sensenbach was not cavalier. It was simply my truth. I had no need to get serious about an acting career. But that didn't stop my passion to learn a craft that, without my awareness, would prepare me to allow another personality to "come through me."

All of our experiences contribute to who we are. It's fun to examine the many ways our passion for one thing may lead us to be comfortable and more efficient in something that does not at first glance seem related.

My realization affirmed my belief that my reluctance to pursue an acting career did not stem from fear of performing in public. I actually took the stage often, but in a completely different capacity. As a child, I loved to dance and had taken my dance lessons quite seriously. When I met Corinne Trabucco Klump, the head of the dance department at Emerson, I hadn't danced in eight years. With Corinne's encouragement, I signed up for a class. Soon, I was taking almost every dance class the department offered. I have to admit, I believe I was neither gifted nor graceful, with one exception. Tap dancing came back to me easily and I loved it. To me, it was another mode of communication: playing music with my feet. Corinne brought me to her teacher, Leon Collins. Before long he asked me to share the stage with him, along with the talented Lady Di, Dianne Walker, and other icons in the field. Leon passed in 1985. His instruction before every routine still echoes in my mind: "One, two, and you know what to do."

After I had not danced for many years and was recovering from a car accident that had cracked my pelvis, he came to me in a dream. The visceral nature of the experience assured me that this was a real visit. He went over a few steps with me and told me that whenever I was ready, he would come to me to help me remember the routines. I have a tap floor in our home, and every once in a while I take out my tap shoes. True to his word, I channel in, "One, two, and you know what to do!"

CHAPTER 15

Living the Truth— Love Is Greater Than Pain

We have explored how embracing the beauty and bounty of the physical world enables us to more easily attune to and interact with the reality of the spiritual plane. Our love for those who are out of body furthers our dedication to embracing the physical world around us. In other words, when we consciously incorporate both the spiritual and physical vibrational realities, one supports the other. The very nature of integrating these dimensional realities raises our consciousness even higher, fine-tuning our sensory and telepathic abilities and broadening the depth of all of our relationships, whether the interaction is with those in body or out. Once you are consciously attuned to vibrating at a higher frequency, you will find that the synchronicities in your life are not arbitrary. As you are drawn to understanding and integrating the active spiritual reality into your daily life, higher-vibrational experiences will manifest more consistently.

It is just the same as the experience of traveling abroad.

Learning some of the local language is sure to enhance every aspect of your trip. Doing so not only allows you to interact with the native population, but it enriches the whole experience. Recognizing similarities and empathizing with others raises our vibration. But there are also practical reasons to learn the language, from discovering local delicacies to finding your way to the closest bathroom.

Happily, learning the language of the spiritual plane is not difficult in the way that we may sometimes experience the intellectual challenge of learning a new language. No specific talent is needed, just the desire to do it. But remember that your soul already knows this language. Too often in our society, the mind is given the primary job of deciphering all discernible incoming information. Of course, your emotion and heart are engaged to help you, as is your instinct. But for many, the common practice is to listen to our mind and logic first. Yet using only the mind to process the soul's dilemmas, expansion, and elevation means using a tool that by its very vibrational nature does not have the capacity for the task.

By merging thoughts with other modes of reception (sensory and vibrational), we help the soul have more comfortable access to the whole vehicle it occupies.

The more we integrate mind, heart, and gut, the more our soul is equipped to access its innate knowledge and develop the best pathways for ongoing communication with loved ones on the out-of-body plane.

This spiritual language only asks that you align your intention with your desire. Ask, whether your need is specific or broad:

- Please help me perceive and incorporate higher vibration.
- Let me feel the reality of my loved one's continued existence.
- Show me signs that I won't miss.

Pour your heart out. Be creative. You know how to do this. You were born with the ability. Acknowledge the part of your physical life and potential that has altered because someone you love has gone to a different vibrational plane. Carry on and grieve because you live in a physical reality and we should never deny that. Feel it, cry for it, and then, as you continue to do that, look up and say "Hello!" Look up and realize that they are already in it with us, reaching out and trying to help. Then, if this is what you desire, learn the language, a language of energy without words that you came into this life knowing. You are capable of doing this. You have done it before. Be patient with yourself and with your out-of-body loved ones. Remember, they may be relearning along with you. If you allow this to be your path, you will become conscious of what interaction has already occurred, and you will expand even further. That wave of energy, the goosebumps, the response of the physical body that you might not have identified before is the high-vibration reaction to the love reaching us from the higher frequency of the spiritual plane.

But if you need help to experience this, or a catalyst to help align you to a higher vibration, there are plenty of in-body people and protocols to help. Ask for help when you need it, from those in body and out. Books, people, groups—help will appear. Just try to keep the door open to the light when you are in the darkest state of despair.

Remember Sophia from Chapter 3? After her daughter, Isabel, passed out of body, she could not connect with the light around her on the physical plane and began to neglect her two sons. As time went on, she retreated further and further, not just from the higher physical vibration, but also from the spiritual one. Thinking that she had let Isabel down made her believe she had let God down. This first step on the downward spiral led Sophia to feel that she had disappointed both God and her loved one, which in turn made her feel that she no longer deserved life, love, or happiness.

As soon as Sophia acknowledged Isabel's continued existence, love, and involvement, everything changed for her. It allowed an opening for Sophia to help herself and her sons and, in so doing, help the daughter she previously thought was out of her reach.

Sophia made the conscious decision to allow her love for her daughter, and her two sons, to be the driving force in her life. While she will still be overwhelmed with pain at times, her embracing of the spiritual realm gives her the courage to re-embrace the family she has on the physical plane. She will, of course, continue to miss her daughter's physical form, but at the same time she is realigning and integrating a more expansive consciousness. She is opening, once again, to life on the Earth plane in an effort to help heal and bring joy and peace to the daughter who has passed.

Don't forget that Sophia was resistant to any kind of help. It's all too easy to feel attached to our pain, since it can feel like the only connection we have to our loved one who has passed. But while you are in that pain, you can still look up and say, "Help me!" That's all it takes to open the door that your loved one is banging on to get through to you.

SOME OF the things we are taught to believe come in when we are not fully cognizant. You may have heard the old joke that we are all looking around us to find God or enlightenment, so Divine Consciousness hides it where we might not look: inside ourselves. But it's not a joke. Divine Consciousness *is* within us. You know all this and much more! Again, we were born with this knowledge. Often, when our lives are going well, there is no desire to incorporate this knowing into our lives on the physical plane. We may not have the impetus until the time comes when we need it the most. The loss of someone we love gives us the opportunity, through our own broken hearts, to remember the spiritual plane and embrace it as a means of survival here on the physical plane. We can integrate the realities of both the physical and spiritual planes while we are still in our physical bodies. This is what is known as enlightenment. When we choose this reality consciously and energetically, we offer our expansion and enlightenment to others. Whatever their belief system, our healing will touch them. Of course, we still love those who choose not to go down this path of integration. But no one else's perception of reality should limit yours. You'll find that if you live your life this way, more and more people who reflect this reality will be drawn to you. Like attracts like. Even if you're not letting your spiritual-reality cat out of the bag conversationally, you are still vibrating at a higher frequency, and people and animals will react to that, whether they are conscious of it or not.

Jack's mom, Celia, asked me why it feels like the energy rises and feels better when I walk into a room. I was not aware that this was so. I looked up and asked Divine Consciousness, "Why?" I channeled in that my energetic presence does indeed change the energy in a room. Interestingly enough, the answer is simply that I asked to change it through my prayer that all I come in contact with will be drawn to God and healed. Remember those prayers or mantras that I use before each reading, as well as in my personal life, for Protection and Intention? Celia's query brought further confirmation that they work!

Once again, here is protection that I use:

"I clothe myself in a robe of light composed of the love, power, and wisdom of God."

Does that prayer resonate for you? If not, feel free to change it up to accommodate your needs and comfort.

I follow up this invocation with the following intention:

"I wear it not only for my own protection, but also so that those who see it, or come in contact with it, will be drawn to God and healed."

I am asking here for healing and protection not only for myself but for those around me. And because my request is answered, any energy that I come into contact with is either already high, or goes higher in response to my request. Any energy or entity that does not want to comply and would rather reside at a lower frequency will not be comfortable in the higher-frequency light, and with the help of Divine Consciousness will move along. Am I conscious that this is happening? Not necessarily. But when I ask Higher Consciousness for support, it is granted. Of course, faith in the universe's support does not take the place of common sense while navigating safely on the physical plane. But as you raise your vibration, you will become more and more aware of this process at work.

Are you powerful enough to do this? Yes! When you set

your intention, you are aligning as a cocreator with Divine Consciousness.

Here's something else to motivate you. Aligning yourself as a cocreator with Divine Consciousness becomes a source of fun! Our out-of-body loved ones, especially children, take great joy in making their family members and friends laugh! When you connect the specific and creative ways that our out-of-body loved ones get through to us and play with us, you realize how aligned their antics are with the personalities that we remember on the Earth plane. As time goes by, you will be better able to differentiate and recognize the energy and personalities of your loved ones.

We Are Deserving

The bottom line is that integration brings joy. When we allow and feel deserving of the reciprocal love that is directed to us from our loved ones on the spiritual plane, we can restore our balance more easily as we navigate our physical lives. Why not make the conscious choice to allow their continuing love to help us? Agreeing to be receptive and let our love flow into our collaboration can bring gifts beyond measure.

It is worth repeating: In an effort to ease our suffering, our loved ones on the spiritual plane will creatively network to align us with more love to be shared on the physical plane. Our out-of-body loved ones want us to be happy, and our happiness brings them great relief. That's what love is about. I can't tell you how many weddings I have attended where I have witnessed an out-of-body husband or wife standing at the side of the bride or groom, while the in-body one stands on the other side.

Love Amplified: From Despair to a New Beginning

Maggie's husband, Barry, passed when their two kids were still pretty young. Barry had had a history of depression, as did other members of his family. He'd struggled with it, had seen doctors, and had taken meds, but sometimes he'd felt there was no avoiding it. A sister had already succumbed and taken her own life. When his doctor took him off his meds with the intention of trying a different combination, he couldn't see his way out of the darkness and took his own life.

Maggie didn't pursue channeling. The connection was made when I was channeling for Jay, who was thirty-one years old and soon to be married.

ME: There's a man here who wants you to give messages to his family. He says you are helping a little brother.

JAY: No, I'm an only child.

BARRY: Your little brother, your little brother! I'm still his father!

Jay's face lit up with understanding. He explained that he belonged to the Big Brother organization and had been paired with Michael for several years.

BARRY: That's my son! I'm his father. I took my life. You have to let him know that I love him! He thinks he wasn't enough for me to want to stay. I wasn't well. I wasn't in my right mind. It isn't anyone's fault. Please, tell him I'm watching over him, his sister, and his mom.

Jay explained that he knew that Michael's dad had taken his life. In fact, the organization had paired them because Jay's dad had done the same thing. Jay was eleven when it happened, Michael was nine. Jay had the personal experience to help Michael and could relate to his "little brother."

Jay shared Barry's information with Michael's mom, Maggie. She called me and I channeled her husband. Maggie and I went on to become friends, and that is how my husband and I came to be at Maggie's wedding to her second husband. As Maggie and her groom, also named Barry, were married, I could clearly see her first husband standing up there with them. Not between them, but next to them.

At the cake-cutting ceremony, Maggie's new husband placed his hand over Maggie's hand. I could then see that Maggie's first husband put his hand on top of both of theirs. The new husband looked puzzled for a second and then smiled. Afterward, he came up to me and asked what I'd seen. He told me he could feel the first husband's hand on top of his own and felt he had his blessing.

The first husband confirmed this later when we channeled.

BARRY: I wanted him to know that I was there and gave my blessing. I love my wife and want her to be happy. If I can't be on the physical plane, I want a good man to be with her. Now our kids have two dads, an out-of-body one and an in-body one. We're a soul family. Don't worry! [He was laughing.] I won't hang around when it's not appropriate.

Years later, I had the honor of attending Michael's wedding. I could see his father standing next to him during the ceremony and sharing in the joy!

OUR OUT-OF-BODY loved ones continue to celebrate the many milestones in our lives, right along with us. So often, children who have passed ask their parents to celebrate their birthday.

"Please, talk about fun stuff. I want to hear you laugh."

"Please get a present you think I'd like. Wrap it up and donate it. That would be so nice and would help all of us."

"Please remember all the sweetness we shared when I was there in body. My being out of body can't erase the joy you had when I was born."

Our loved ones on the spiritual plane love to be acknowledged. We can reminisce and treasure our physical-life memories. When we allow ourselves to also continue our relationships in real time, we can celebrate and share not just our past, but also our own ongoing commitment to growth and to each other.

I will always be grateful to Elie Wiesel. His generosity with his time and his counsel truly guided me to be comfortable in my own skin. Like so many of his students, I wanted him to know how profoundly he affected me. I happily watched over the years, as former students gifted him with their achievements. Someday I will write about my personal experiences with him, I thought, and maybe that will be my way to thank him.

I pictured it, I dreamed about it, and in 2016 he passed. He didn't know of my intention before he passed, but he certainly learned about it later. Not long after he transitioned out of his physical body, he came to me. I could see him clearly and experienced that familiar feeling of his kindness and warmth. I then realized that something was in my hands. I could physically feel the texture with my fingers. It felt soft, but with hard things inside of it. I looked down, and in my hands was a beautifully embroidered tallit bag, the traditional protective covering for a Jewish prayer shawl. I moved my fingers and was surprised to find that there were books inside. I was puzzled, until I looked up into my dear teacher's eyes. There I saw the understanding and love that many of us felt so lucky and grateful to receive. He smiled and nodded. Without hesitation, I held out the bag. Still looking into my eyes, he accepted it and held it to his heart. He nodded once again. And then he was gone. He took the gift with him. I was overwhelmed with relief and gratitude.

Eating the Apples

In my younger days, when I realized that my channeling could help people, I would feel guilty when I wasn't doing it. This, of course, didn't lead to a balanced life. I came up with the analogy that people needed apples and I could deliver them. To be the best apple-delivery person that I could be, I understood that I couldn't do it all the time. But there were so many people who needed apples. Eventually I became aware of when it might be best to rest my voice, or just rest in general. I thought this was all it took to take care of myself.

When I was growing (not going) through the cancer experience a few years ago, I noticed for the first time that I only channeled for other people, never for myself. Of course I knew I was guided and protected, as I always asked to be when I would channel for others. But I never specifically asked for help and clarity on a personal level. Cancer was the impetus, and my need was great.

I looked up and asked for help.

The answer I received felt as if it had come from deep inside me. The message felt like something I had once known but had forgotten.

"You have to eat the apples."

What?

"You have to eat the apples!"

I started to laugh. How obvious!

I found the extent of my unconsciousness hilarious. Being allowed to channel for others did not automatically mean that I was channeling for myself. Of course I had many spontaneous visits from out-of-body family and friends and appreciated all their help. But though I would look up and ask for their help for others, I never asked for it for myself.

I looked up to my out-of-body loved ones and guides.

"I have to eat the apples!"

Just like Dorothy in *The Wizard of Oz*, who discovers that she has always carried within her the answer she has been seeking, I'd had the ability to channel for myself all along. Divine Consciousness informed me that they, like the Good Witch, had always known this truth, but like Dorothy, I'd needed to have my own growth experience to bring this revelation to consciousness.

I'd had to earn it. And I did this by consciously asking for help. The correlation of the apple and knowledge is not lost on me.

Divine Consciousness knows that we are here to learn and grow. While they guide us to the highest good, it is up to us to allow ourselves the expansion and insight we need to accomplish what we came here to do.

As I looked up and continued to laugh at the obvious, I heard from loving guides, "That's why we gave you the apple analogy to begin with!"

I was astounded. "What? That whole apple thing was channeled?"

"Yes, we tried to help you. We knew you would get it when you needed it."

So, PLEASE be good to yourself and eat the apples.

WHEN WE do eat the apples, and allow ourselves to receive, experience, and appreciate the bounty and love of both the physical and spiritual planes, we realize that we are worthy of all the love that surrounds us. The ongoing communication with our loved ones helps us to embrace, with purpose and joy, our physical life. If we allow ourselves to expand our spiritual reality to include what we may or may not initially perceive, we live in the higher frequency that nourishes the whole of our being.

ALL OF us have difficult periods of grief. But when we resonate with who we really are, beautiful spiritual beings choosing growth through a physical experience, we align with truth and joy.

This happened when I was asleep, but it was more than a dream. I had a visceral and real experience on the spiritual plane.

I WAS surrounded by high-vibrational beings. People refer to them as angels, archangels, and avatars. It was pure joy as we mingled and played. Then I saw an elevator door open. All of the beautiful light beings floated into the elevator. I saw that it was crowded, and I wasn't sure what I was supposed to do. Should I squeeze in with them, as this was what I truly wanted to do? In that split second of hesitation, the door closed, and the elevator ascended without me. I was devastated. My heart sank as I thought that I had missed my opportunity.

Just then, I heard the laughter of my ethereal playmates. I closed my eyes and listened. Joy returned, and to my astonishment, I felt myself rise. And there I was, once again in the company of my high-vibration guides and friends.

They embraced me as I realized that they had just taught me the reality of my own capability. I didn't need an elevator. And neither did they. They'd simply used it as a tool to teach me. My soul had known how to access the higher-vibrational level all along.

We are all capable. At our low points, it helps to remind ourselves who we are . . . who we really are.

Who are we?

We are cocreators, sharers, and healers of high-vibrational Divine Consciousness.

EACH DAY, as we consciously choose to live in truth, love emerges as the continuing undying force. We knew this when we came into the physical plane, and we are reminded of it when we return to the spiritual plane. When we resonate with this reality, we rise to our highest potential and align with our soul's wisdom, truly knowing that Love Is Greater Than Pain.

Epilogue

On a Sunday morning, as Harry and I were on our way out for breakfast, I suddenly channeled in a declaration from spiritual guides.

"Random House isn't random!
Your books will come out through Random House!"

I repeated the words to Harry. While we were happy to hear this, it felt a bit random!

The only other time I'd received channeled guidance regarding my writing was almost ten years earlier. I was working on a book, not this one, and the agent who was representing it had submitted it to various publishers. When one of them offered to put together a two- to three-book deal, I heard a definitive "No!" from my guides. While I wanted the book published, I knew enough to listen to spiritual guidance. As usual, Harry backed me up, as did my agent.

Years went by. My attention was directed to the health challenges of family members, and eventually my own.

A COUPLE of years later, Harry and I attended a lecture given by the memoirist Victor Villaseñor. We had come to know him personally after I channeled for his sister, Sita Paloma. I had no idea they were related until Sita, after the first time I channeled for her, asked if she could invite her brother over to meet me. Harry and I had read all of his books, and when I told Victor that we were originally from Boston, he told us that his editor, Jill Kramer, had gone to school in Boston.

Jill Kramer? I knew that name! She had gone to Boston University with me! Before the talk, Victor brought Jill over to meet Harry and me. "Here's your old friend!" he said. Jill and I looked at each other, and though we didn't immediately recognize each other, we reminisced enough to realize that we'd had the same major, communications, and had graduated from Boston University in the same year.

Jill and I had a lot in common. As editorial director at Hay House for eighteen years, she understood a lot about the spiritual world. We got together for dinner, and as we talked, I began to remember Jill from our college years. I mentioned that she still had the same beautiful blonde hair. Jill started to laugh. "Now I know why I didn't really recognize you. You think I'm the other Jill Kramer!" I was puzzled. Jill explained that there was another Jill Kramer who had gone to Boston University with us. She had been blonde, and the blonde Jill in front of me had been a brunette in college.

. . .

MEANWHILE, I completed the book I was working on and started this one. I was unsure of the best way to publish them.

Shortly after going through the hardest part of my cancer experience, I looked up and asked Divine Consciousness what to do. "If these books are supposed to get out there and help people, please show me the way. I'll do whatever you think best."

Divine Consciousness works fast! The next day, I received an email from Maribeth Bandas. She explained that we had met at a gathering at a mutual friend's home. I had done some channeling for a few of the people there, so my memory of the social part of the evening was a bit sketchy. Maribeth asked if I was working on any writing projects. She explained that she was an editor, and was also interested in having a channeling session. She wondered if we might work together.

I looked up, laughed, and said, "Wow, God, you work fast!"

MARIBETH EDITED the first book I had written, as I continued to work on this one. I was grateful that Divine Consciousness had brought us together. Her insight and talent are eclipsed only by her warmth and humor; and she and her husband, Hector Ericksen-Mendoza, became our close friends.

By this point, Jill was no longer at Hay House and was now a literary agent at Waterside Productions. She and I had begun getting together regularly with a small group of like-minded ladies, self-dubbed The *Source*resses (pun intended). The day after Maribeth's email, I was meeting with this group when suddenly Alan presented himself. I had recently channeled him for his mom, Fay. Alan asked me to share with the Sourceresses what he had told his mother, that we come here to learn that "Love Is Greater Than

Pain." When I spoke those words aloud, I was surprised to feel Jill's hand on mine and hear her say, "That is the name of your book. May I represent you?"

I heard Alan laugh, along with the guides, as I looked up again. My gratitude was overwhelming.

I TOLD Jill about the Random House information I had downloaded years before. While intrigued, she still sent the proposal for *Love Is Greater Than Pain* to all the big publishers. Gail Gonzales from Rodale was interested. I interviewed and channeled with her. Jill began negotiating with her, but the process came to a halt when Hearst purchased Rodale. Hearst kept the magazine division, then sold the book division to Random House.

"Aha!" we thought. "There it is." But no, that was not the way it happened.

There were some interesting manifestations happening. I noticed an email in my inbox from another publisher asking for more information about my book. When I opened it to read it, the email disappeared. I called Jill and asked if she had forwarded the email to me. She had not. She checked her inbox and had not yet had any correspondence from that particular publisher. A couple of hours later, she called back. She had just received an email from that publisher asking for more information! He had not tried to contact me earlier.

As the book journey unfolded, Jill got into the habit of telling me that one day we would truly understand why *Love Is Greater Than Pain* was taking such a circuitous route. She was right.

Cindy Spiegel, from Random House's Spiegel & Grau imprint, got in touch with Jill after reading the proposal. We interviewed by phone. Though I'd enjoyed interviewing with and channeling for the other publishers, I knew immediately that the book had found its home. Cindy started by saying, "I'm not sure why I feel I should tell you this, but I edited *The Color of Water*." An energetic affirmative wave passed through me. "You're telling me," I answered, "because it is one of my all-time-favorite books! I just finished reading it again! It holds up after twenty years!"

Before we knew it, Jill invited Harry and me to join her for dinner. We chatted for a while. I looked down at the menu, and when I looked back up, Jill was holding up a sign.

> You were right.
> Random House is not random!
> Spiegel & Grau is your new publisher!
> Congrats!!!

Harry and I were ecstatic. I thought of Cindy and again felt the affirmative wave of energy.

THE BOOK contract went back and forth, as contracts do. On the day it was finalized, Harry and I went to the post office like a couple of giddy kids. We both had to be touching the envelope as we pushed it through the mail slot.

Once we got home, I was preparing to go out for the evening with visions of book covers dancing in my head. I kept seeing images of trees. Meanwhile, Harry, who was ready to go and waiting for me, picked up one of the books that Cindy had published and had kindly sent to us. When I came downstairs, Harry excitedly called me over. "You have to see this!" In his hand was a copy of

The Man Who Planted Trees: A Story of Lost Groves, the Science of Trees, and a Plan to Save the Planet by Jim Robbins, a science reporter for the *New York Times*. Harry showed me the paragraph that had grabbed his heart and attention. It was about David Milarch, a Michigan arborist who'd had a near-death experience years ago. When he returned to the physical plane, he had the ability to channel archangels. He was told he had a mission: he was directed to go to the oldest, strongest champion trees in the world, retrieve the freshest DNA, create clones, and repopulate the world with the trees that are necessary to continue our earthly survival. If the champion trees go, they told him, everything else would go, too. David's out-of-body experience put him on a path to save the world.

As I read about David, I could feel the familiar affirmative energetic wave. "This is amazing!" I told Harry. Just the day before I'd channeled for a man whose wife had passed. She had been an avid gardener while in her physical body. The husband asked if she could still enjoy her favorite hobby now that she was on the spiritual plane. The wife had then launched into an exciting description of how she is now working with others, in body and out, to clone and grow the trees needed to ensure our continuing earthly existence. While she was channeling in, I did something I'd never done before. I don't usually remember what I channel, but as I heard her words, I knew I needed to remember them. I stopped the recorder and explained to the husband that I was intrigued by what his wife was saying. Would it be all right with him if I asked Divine Consciousness to allow me to remember all that came in about the trees? He replied, "Of course." I then continued channeling. That is how I was able to recall the information when Harry showed me the book. I looked up and said, "Thank you," as I marveled at the synchronicity. I felt a warm hug of energy as I channeled in a guide's response:

> "Yes, the synchronicity is lovely. Now, let us tell you ex-actly what is going on."

"We channeled in 'Random House isn't random. Your books will come out through Random House.' We needed to direct you to Cindy Spiegel so that you could work on this project and chan-nel with and for David Milarch. We have been preparing and di-recting you."

As I listened, I felt wave after wave of high-frequency energy. I had just been picturing the book cover and was thinking that I needed to tell Cindy I was hoping for a tree on the jacket. I grew up just south of Boston, by a forest adjacent to the Blue Hills. As a child, I could be found, weather permitting, deep in the forest, or in a tree with a book.

THE GUIDES CONTINUED: We needed to wait until your contract was signed before we could give you this information. Now that it's all set, you can call Cindy and share all of this with her.

I LOVED the integrity of the information coming in. We have free will. Cindy took on *Love Is Greater Than Pain* because she liked the book. My potential channeling for the tree project was not a factor. I couldn't wait to share what I'd learned with her. And I couldn't wait to tell Jill. I realized how right she had been all along, that one day we would find out exactly why the book was landing where it did.

Cindy, upon hearing what I had to share, told me that she'd in-stinctively known that it was imperative for *The Man Who Planted Trees* to reach the public. She was now on the board of David Mi-larch's nonprofit, Archangel Ancient Tree Archive. David estab-lished the organization in order to physically manifest his mission to save our planet by planting trees. In fact, an expedition to climb and take clippings to clone champion sequoias in California was being planned, and Cindy suggested that Harry and I come along.

Again, I got the affirmative energetic wave.

IN NOVEMBER of 2018, during California's devastating fires, we joined Cindy, David, and his merry band of brilliant scientists and climbers at Camp Nelson. Our plans were precarious, as the air quality was pretty bad and the wind kept shifting the many fires' directions.

An "elevator" was set up, and we had the opportunity to go to the top of one of the tallest known trees in the world. The elevator was in fact a pulley system, one rope attached to a harness. You sat in the harness and were pulled up the tree while another person came down.

Harry looked at the disclaimer we had to sign before going up. He's a lawyer, so I thought it was the beginning of the end. Instead, he said, "Just sign it! If we read it, we won't do it." I watched in amazement as he harnessed up and ascended! I was his counter-weight, and as I went up, I passed him as he was on his way down. I thought that was so romantic—meeting halfway up a sequoia like that. We could look into each other's eyes during this life-altering experience. But no, it was not to be, as Harry got his rope en-tangled in mine, and we ended up spinning away from each other!

We both landed safely, along with Cindy and everyone else who ventured up well over two hundred feet to the top of the tree. It was a beautiful experience, especially after the initial thirty seconds of panic. David's crew knew exactly how to support us, literally and figuratively.

The only thing that felt "higher" than going to the top of the tree was channeling with David. Energetic sparks were flying. His high-frequency energy felt contagious. Everyone who was involved was joyfully determined to save the trees and save the world. And, Harry and I met Cindy Spiegel in person. It felt like a family reunion, another gift.

The morning we were to leave, I felt an overwhelming desire to stay. The people, the energy, the purpose . . . it was a natural high. I felt the warm energetic hug of Divine Consciousness and heard this message: "As hard as it is to leave this beautiful forest and new friends, leaving is an important part of the plan. You are all entrusted to bring Archangel Ancient Tree Archive's message to the world." You are invited to be on board. Go to ancienttreearchive.org.

After we returned home, David and I channeled several times over the phone. He invited us to the next expedition. In May of 2019, we went to Crescent City, California, to climb the redwoods. David and his team again gifted us with another life-changing and life-affirming experience. We went to the top of one of the tallest redwoods. Once again, the natural high frequency of the people involved, including Cindy and David, matched the exhilarating energy of the climb. As we hiked the Jedediah Smith Trail in the nearby national forest, I was reminded of my childhood passion. Surrounded by trees, I felt at home. I could feel the presence of Archangels.

Random House was certainly not random. I realize now that I have been receiving information and aligning with trees my whole life.

The trees are a lot like us. They are all connected. They communicate through their root systems, and also energetically. They are telepathic and have empathic responses to one another. They instinctively know that they are in this life together. Trees are also alchemists. They absorb light, water, and carbon dioxide, giving us precious oxygen, along with many other gifts. We are also alchemists! We learn from our earthly experiences and resonate with emotion. Then we have a choice. When we recognize and process pain, yet choose love and growth as our purpose, we transform ourselves and each other!

There has been yet another curious twist at the end of the story of this book's publication. Just after I handed in the manuscript for the book, Spiegel & Grau was a casualty in a corporate restructuring. Cindy left Random House, though she generously continued to edit my book, and the book moved to the imprint Harmony. Donna Loffredo is now the editor and publisher of *Love Is Greater Than Pain*. I appreciate her enthusiasm and know that her involvement is far from random.

I believe that Divine Consciousness created the networking, employing in-body and out-of-body resources, to bring me where I was supposed to be. Nothing was random. I hope my sharing a part of this book's journey shines a light on all the things that are not random in your life. I believe there is networking and intention guiding each and every one of us. Every soul has a sacred purpose and has come here bravely.

Like the trees, we're all in this together.

Acknowledgments

There is a Divine Conspiracy that we are all a part of. We are collaborators in this beautiful life experience, whether we draw breath on the Earth plane or we resonate with the vibrational energy out of body.

I didn't realize how much writing this book would heal my own heart. Throughout this book process, the Divine Conspiracy swept me up, leading me to people who resonate on a soul level and into a deeper relationship with those already in my life.

It doesn't just take a village, it takes a universe.

I'd like to express my appreciations to so many who share my world.

Harry, my wonderful husband, would come home from work, throw together dinner because most likely I had not, and then sit for hours typing my handwritten, often-scrambled, chapters. He is obviously a very patient man, as well as compassionate and kind. Oh, and brilliant and funny, too. You'll type the next one, right? Thank you, Harry, for being my rock and wrangler. We are a soul team on this journey, and our shared sense of wonder has never waned. You are the definition of love and integrity.

Our children, Zak, Jesse, and Sarah. Thank you for your love and support.

Zak, thank you for your questions and research. I appreciate and honor your compassion, integrity, and quick wit.

Jesse, your authenticity, wry sense of humor, and talent are a heady combination. Thank you for your awesome and creative music, clarity, and thoughtful insight.

Sarah, your beauty, inside and out, and your brilliance are eclipsed only by your kindness and generosity. How I love that magnificent voice, lifting us up, whether you're singing or sharing your truth.

My parents, Agnes and Sam Margolies. Because of you, I believe in magic and always knew that the magic was a day-to-day affair. Your door was always open. There was room and love for all who came our way. I chose well; and I appreciate your ongoing guidance, humor, and love.

My brother, Mark Margolies. Maybe all that bullying we endured when we were kids taught us to listen to our own melody and gave us the courage to pursue what really matters. Your music was the steady soundtrack of my youth and brought me more joy than you can imagine. Thank you for your support on so many levels.

Sometimes the best is worth waiting for. Mark is now playing duets with Jane Zwerneman, the continually inspiring and talented sister-in-love I have always dreamed of. We're blessed that our families have come together.

∞

Cindy Spiegel and Julie Grau, thank you for saying "Yes!"

Cindy Spiegel, you are truly the fairy godmother of this project. I'm sure many of your authors feel the same way. Thank you beyond words for your generosity and talent. Your brilliance, vision, and direction gave me the confidence to convey my truth in a way I never thought possible. The world is a sweeter, richer place because you are in it. Thank you for shining your light on where we need to focus our attention. You really are a pure conduit of the angels.

Donna Loffredo, thank you for your enthusiasm and insight. I'm delighted that your vision is aligned with my intention. Your buoyant energy brings joy to every step of the process.

Thank you, Harmony and Random House, including Gail Gonzales and the great team: Katherine Leak, Diana Baroni, Brianne Sperber, Christina Foxley, Lindsey Kennedy, Tammy Blake, Heather Williamson, and Joyce Wong.

Jill Kramer, dear friend and agent, I am so grateful for your wisdom, enthusiasm, and support. Thank you, Victor Villaseñor, for bringing us back together. What fun we're having watching this saga unfold, and how deeply sweet it is as we continue to learn who we are. Thank you for sharing the vision and being uniquely qualified as the right person to bring this book where it needed to be.

Bill Gladstone, thank you for your part in bringing this book to light and for your perfect timing.

Maribeth Bandas, without consciously realizing it, you heard my plea and answered the call. Your compassion, kindness, and talent complement your deep insight. Thank you and your husband, Hector Ericksen-Mendoza, for all of your help, support, friendship, and for sharing this beautiful life with us.

Hillary Kohnke-Sunenshine and Alex Kohnke, thank you for your friendship, hospitality, and support. From logo design to website design, I appreciate your talent and generosity. May our families continue to enjoy many holidays together.

David Milarch, thank you for your insight, humor, heart, and for not being afraid of taking on your mission. Though we met last year on the physical plane, we've been working together for a long time, and our collaboration continues. What fun it is to share that high vibration!

Thank you to everyone involved with Archangel Ancient Tree Archive. We appreciate everything you are doing to ensure the earth's future. We are in awe of your expertise and contagious confidence, allowing Harry and I, along with so many others, to have a sacred tree-climbing experience.

Thank you, Josh Lehrer, for your kindness and generosity to the project and to us.

Robin Lippin, when I asked my mother if she thought it was appropriate to ask you to be a bridesmaid at my wedding, even though I had known you for just a couple of years, she told me to follow my heart. "Yes," she said, "you will always be friends, and Robin will play a major role in your life." Insightful words considering you became a casting director. You are gifted, helping everyone step into the "role" that will expand their greatest potential and growth. It's no wonder that you are so great at your job when this is who you are as a person. I appreciate you, your vision, your kindness, and your humor.

Thank you to so many of your friends, including Rachelle and Ed Begley and Jo and Bill La Mond, for their generosity and joyful inclusiveness.

Sita Paloma Villaseñor, dear MamaSita, together we joyfully dance, play, rejoice, and share the Divine Conspiracy to spread the light. I continue to learn so much from you. Your insight and generosity have helped me expand my collaboration with Divine Consciousness. Your intuitive and powerful bodywork keeps me on my feet. You bring joy, beauty, and balance to the world, and I'm so grateful we are in this life together. Plus, we sure are having a whole lot of fun!

Thank you, Victor Villaseñor, Linda Villaseñor, and Barbara Villaseñor for your generous encouragement, insight, and advice. We love being part of your extended family.

Idelle Kehoe, dear Tanta, we share a distinctly sweet soul connection, manifesting physically and spiritually. You baked cakes for our mitzvahs, and together we started "Chosen Chocolates." You were the creative genius and I merely took direction. However, you couldn't have had a more enthusiastic "taster." After my recent surgery, you hopped on a plane, went straight to the store, and commenced to make a cheesecake. I appreciate your generosity, magnificent voice, and hilarious sense of humor (except of course when it hurts too much to laugh!). Together we grew used to our out-of-body visitors and shared visions. My heart and soul are grateful that we are in this life together. And thank you, Ed Kehoe. We appreciate your sense of humor, kindness, and generosity.

Enid and Alan Rutstein, thank you for your generosity and insight. Enid, dear friend, thank you for your support and help during my many medical adventures. I can't begin to count how many doctors' appointments and chemotherapy sessions you sat through; and my heart can't measure the love, learning, and fun we continue to share.

Jessica Schwartz, thank you for your friendship, insight, beautiful voice, and support. You have a unique way of magnifying the beauty and magic around you, shining a light on the sacred.

Betty Jampel shares my husband's holocaust family background. Out of the history of ashes come those who rise up and tend to the deepest needs of those around them. As a social worker, you are a skilled midwife, helping souls transition back to spirit with consciousness and compassion. Thank you for your generosity and friendship.

Janet Whitney, your wisdom, generosity, and support have helped me grow on so many levels. You are an amazing woman, and I appreciate you and treasure our ongoing friendship.

Marie Moore, what fun we're having as our paths unfold. Thank you for the clarity, insight, and empowerment you bring to the world.

Irene Weinberg, thank you for being a dynamic force, bringing hope and support to those who grieve.

Thank you, Jewels Johnson and The Law of Attraction Talk Radio, and thank you, Dee Wallace, for bringing us together. I appreciate the light and insight you both bring to the world.

Thank you, Ken Druck, for the beautiful work you do. You are truly an insightful and deep healer.

Thank you, dear Book Group: Ruth Berg, Robbie Kirshner, and Lee Aven. I appreciate our shared sweet determination as we explored and expanded. We learned so much together.

Thank you, dear Sourceresses (misspelling intended): Jill Kramer, Cathy Patrick, and Hillary Kohnke-Sunenshine. Thank you for your kindness, generosity, and magic.

Thank you, dear Lamplighters: Sita Paloma, Stephanie, Jenna, Maribeth, Cathy, Hillary, Michele, Kimberly, Vanessa, Phyllis, Glenna, and all who come with the intention of expanding light and consciousness.

Thank you to Enid and Alan's loving and inclusive neighbors.

∞

And thank you to:

Elie Wiesel
Albert Einstein

Wayne Dyer
Louise Hay
Lucille Ball
Leon Collins
Sathya Sai Baba
My "tribunal," including the Baal Shem Tov and Rabbi
   Nachman
And to so many others, for your loving support.

Thank you, Congregation Beth Am and Rabbis David Kornberg and Matthew Earne for your wisdom, generosity, and support.

Billy Galewood, thank you and your pals, Jason Mraz and MC Flow, for bringing us joy and laughter when we really could use it, and for making this world a better place.

Lisa Buchanan, bosom buddy, thank you for your friendship and generosity; and thank you, along with Cindy Hill Infante and Jane Jewell, for your camaraderie and support.

We are grateful to:

The Hameed and Farivar families, especially Afsaneh, Amir,
   Talla, Amean, Anne, Emean, Shireen, Richelle Damavandi
   Stowe, and Matthew
The Ivey Family: Nancy, Murph, Charlotte, Maria, and Murphy
The Koerner family: Kip, Karen, Allyson, Brooke, and Ryan
The Schulman family: Suzanne, Paul, Jenna, and Todd
The Cardenas family: especially George, Virginia, John, and April
The Jones family: Kerri, Johnnie, Mikaela, and Alex
Rabbi Julie Wolkoff and Bob Weiner

Denise and Al Roberts

Judi and Len Margolis

Adam Green

Susan Mullins and Noam Pitlik

Robin Norwood

Brie Burkeman

Bob Harbin

Magdalena, Kirk, and Tito Whisler

Susan Jansen

Caroline and Peter Courtnage

The Younger family, especially Tim. I appreciate your
kindness and generosity and will continue to pay it
forward.

Susan Kelley

Debbie and Bernie Waggenheim

Shelley and Syd Baron

Stephanie and Ed Valanzola

Corinne Trabucco and Jack Benedetto

Karen Robbins

Patty Huang and Bill Schmidt

The Goszczycki family

Judy and David Sawyer, Odessa Sawyer-Irish

Tracy Porterfield

Stephanie Fletcher Robinson and Jeffrey

Laura Kurdi

Ramsey Kurdi

Melanie Ross and Mark Grover

Sandy and Randy Clark and Jon Willmschen

Rosey and Mark Robbins

Leanne and Jim Rand
Phyllis Nofts and Evelyn Ray
Donna and Jess Freher-Lyons
Susanne Kende

Thank you to everyone I have channeled for, and everyone I have channeled, for allowing me to be your conduit.

I realize that my language here is repetitive. How often can you use the words *insight, kindness, generosity,* and *wisdom? This many,* because I'm sharing the truth!

Thank you to all my family and friends who have been my joy and support over the years.

I have been blessed with the help and expertise of many in the healing profession. I thank all and want to acknowledge the kindness of a few who went above and beyond.

Dr. Mark Sherman met with Harry and me during his lunchtime between surgeries. I'll never forget when I opened my eyes after the first surgery and saw Harry's joyful face and yours, as you looked over his shoulder. Your expression told me all I needed to know, as well as so much about your own heart.

Dr. Spencer Schaeffer, thank you for all your help. You taught my body how to maintain its structural integrity, and we had fun doing it. I have no doubt that you are working your magic and teaching in-body doctors the subtlety and strength of your talent.

Dr. Bridgette Duggan, thank you for the loving care you gave to my mom and me. We can honestly say that you've saved generations.

Dr. Tom Thrall, thank you for your healing talent and generosity.

My heart still resonates with your advice to keep things "light" and pay it forward.

Corinne Trabucco, dear friend, thank you for dance classes, bringing me to Leon Collins, all that wonderful Alexander Technique; and assuring me, many years ago, that eventually spiritual conversations will be the norm.

Shannon Kleinman, you are a true and compassionate healer. Thank you for your wonderful acupuncture and for sharing this beautiful, magical journey.

Kim Taylor, thank you and thanks to all the generous acupuncturists who volunteered their time to help cancer patients.

Eileen Troberman, thank you for your sweetness and for your Alexander Technique talent.

Tamara Branden, nutritionist and acupuncturist, thank you for your wisdom and keeping us in line (as much as we allow you to!).

Beatriz Lewis, oncology pharmacist extraordinaire, you are a ray of sunshine in a place where we really need it. Thank you for your upbeat sweetness and keeping everything organized.

Thank you, Divine Consciousness. I am so grateful. As the synchronicities unfold, it feels like a state of grace.

Thank you for reading this book. I wish you healing, joy, expansion, and peace.

About the Author

Marilyn Kapp is a spiritual medium who had her first experience communicating with those who passed when she was just two years old. At Boston University, Kapp studied with Elie Wiesel, who became a friend and mentor. Kapp went on to receive a master of arts from Emerson College. Kapp has performed thousands of personal readings for individuals and families, conducting sessions all over the United States and internationally in person and by telephone. You can visit Marilyn at marilynkapp.com.